EZEKIEL'S AMERICA

Keith Fee

To Wayne and Trish Egan Two good Friends

Outskirts Press, Inc.
Denver, Colorado

7/9/06

Ezekiel's America
All Rights Reserved
Copyright © 2006 Keith Fee

Outskirts Press
http://www.outskirtspress.com

ISBN-10: 1-59800-415-8
ISBN-13: 978-1-59800-415-1

Library of Congress Control Number: 2006922440

Outskirts Press and the "OP" logo are trademarks belonging to
Outskirts Press, Inc.

Printed in the United States of America

CHAPTER One
Ezekiel's America

A ncient prophets have made promises and predictions throughout the Bible revealing events that will happen in the latter days leading up to the end of this earth age that greatly concerns and involves America and other nations around the world. Some prophecy has not been taught by our modern day clergy that could have very important effects upon the whole earth.

Ezekiel, one of the greatest prophets of the Old Testament, has confirmed what we have feared for some time; that Russia, along with a host of her confederates, will invade America - our land. A heretofore unknown warning is that this catastrophic event will take place at some time in the near future. It could happen at any time.

Russia and her allies will be defeated. Eighty-three percent of her forces will be destroyed!

Most clergy think this will be an attack upon the tiny Jewish state of Israel in the middle east by Russia and her confederates. We will prove this assumption is in dangerous error and can not possibly be today's Jewish nation called Israel!

This prophecy is not new, but has always been included in the Bible. It has been avoided because clergy and Bible teachers do not understand it. Finally, we have discovered the meaning of this prophecy and how it involves America as we carefully explore the words and characteristics of true Israel by the prophet Ezekiel.

The prophecy characterizes Israel as a land that does not in any manner describe today's little Israel in the middle east! Very few of today's clergy, teachers and Bible scholars have understood the open descriptions of the land to be invaded by Russia. Ezekiel is readily describing the exact prophetic characteristics in easy to understand terms one must find in true Israel! These characteristics are included in the prophecy to enable us to determine the true Israel. Israel absolutely must meet these descriptions or the bible is wrong !

The Time is Right for our Understanding

That this prophecy involves America will surprise many. Not all Bible students and clergy take time to read into prophecy, but rather glide over and ignore all prophecies they do not fully understand or that would affect the doctrines of their belief. Perhaps the time has come that the Lord has opened up our understanding of the words of this prophecy. As you may recall, there was a time recorded in the book of Daniel when the Lord instructed Daniel to seal the words of the book for the time was not ripe (Daniel 12:4):

"But thou, O Daniel, shut up the words, and seal the book, *even* to the time of the end; many shall run to and fro, and knowledge shall be increased."

2

It's very possible our knowledge has finally been increased that we can read and place proper significance to the words and descriptions of this prophecy. As we draw nearer to the time of the end, we are seeing many things being opened to our understanding. Many of us have experienced this quality to some degree as we have read and re-read scripture we could not at first understand and finally it jumps right out in front of our eyes!

We will prove, through the ease of understanding the words of this prophecy, that Ezekiel can not be describing the tiny state of Israel in the middle east.

Although not named, the United States is identified numerous times in the Bible by their own particular characteristics. The ancient prophets of the Bible did not know the names of future civilizations nor of the western world at the time the Bible was being written. Because of prophetic events to take place involving western nations, there is more than ample prophecy in the Bible to identify America and other western nations. Today's ministers and teachers say America is not mentioned in the Bible. The word America surely is not mentioned, but the description of America is given in many places through prophecies of the end times. Else the Bible would be incomplete since it would not include the greatest nations of the world.

The Northern Ten Tribes of Israel

The Northern Ten Tribes of Israel were originally part of the House of Israel which included all of the twelve tribes of Israel under the rule of David and later his son Solomon. Because of the sins of Solomon, the House of Israel was divided up into two Kingdoms:

- After the division, the tribe of Judah, which included

the tribe of Benjamin were headquartered in Jerusalem and constituted the Kingdom of Judah.

- The other kingdom consisted of the Northern Ten Tribes of Israel which were headquartered in Samaria. Because the Northern Ten Tribes included the birth-right holders, they became the Kingdom of Israel, they were very massive in number - in the millions! The birthright holders of Israel were Joseph's two sons, Ephraim and Manasseh. They were included in the northern tribes.

There were now two Kingdoms; The Kingdom of Judah, head-quartered in Jerusalem and the Kingdom of Israel known as the Northern Ten Tribes, headquartered in Samaria. The King-dom of Israel in Samaria was taken captive in 721 BC. The Kingdom of Judah in the south was not taken captive at the same time as the massive Northern Ten Tribes.

The Northern Ten Tribes after being taken captive were even-tually scattered throughout all of the nations of the world; thus fulfilling the prophecy of Amos 9:9:

"For, lo, I will command, and I will sift the house of Israel among all nations, like as *corn* is sifted in a sieve, yet shall not the least grain fall upon the earth."

And as we shall see, Israel was sifted throughout _all_ nations upon the face of the earth to include the seven continents of the world. You can be assured when you consider any nation on the earth, there will also be members of the House of Israel re-siding there! God will mark the members of the house of Israel as stated above: "…Yet shall not the least grain fall upon the earth."

The two kingdoms - Kingdom of Judah and Kingdom of Israel - still remain separate and will be reunited at the time of the return of the Lord to set up his kingdom on earth (Ezek. 37).

The Northern Ten Tribes in Samaria were under the rule of Jeroboam. They set up their own government and their own temple worship changing some of beliefs and traditions previously practiced by the Israelites. They adopted idol worship. For this, God gave them over to the Assyrians in 721 BC, who took them captive.

The Northern Ten Tribes lived in slavery to their Assyrians invaders until they, along with the Assyrians, were driven further north by the Medes. There they crossed the Caucasus mountains into the Crimean region north of the Black Sea where they lived in exile for a time; finally migrating east and west. The main migration eventually went west to the European nations. Parts of Israel spread east from the Crimean area into the far eastern Asian regions. Some of the Tribe of Dan escaped the captivity in Assyria by ship and went to the extreme western European nations of what is today's Great Britain, Scotland and Ireland.. Others were also driven south of the Black Sea and through Greece into southern Europe.

The Lost Tribes of Israel

The Ten Tribes of Israel were not destroyed as some clergy and Bible students would teach and have you believe, but they were scattered to the nations as ancient prophets forewarned (Amos 9:9). Today they inhabit many countries of the earth in huge numbers; in the hundreds of millions! Because they abandoned the commandment regarding the true Sabbath Day worship, no longer observed the covenant of their God and began idol worship, they lost their identity as the Kingdom of Israel.

Although some Bible scholars agree they are located on earth, most don't know who or where they are today. They became known as the Ten Lost Tribes of Israel! The Lost Tribes are alive and well on earth today and are the prominent nations of the world. We will show you where some of the tribes mentioned above are to be found on earth today!

The Ten Lost Tribes are not to be confused with the tiny Jewish state in the middle east called Israel. The ten tribes do not reside there at this time. A mistake most clergy of the protestant world make is assuming the Jews constitute the whole house of Israel. And, of course, they most emphatically do not. This is wrong and we will prove it within this book.

Some of the Jews have returned to their homeland but the re-gathering has barely started. There will be many millions of Israelites in their homeland before the re-gathering can be completed. The land area that will eventually include and be home to the full Twelve Tribes of Israel will expand to cover a vast area including the land presently being occupied by others including the Palestinians and other countries in the Middle East. In short, the full house of Israel will occupy the land they owned before being taken captive, separated, and scattered around the world.

Ezekiel's Mission

In the year 589 B.C. an invasion of Jerusalem took place. This was not the main Invasion and destruction of Jerusalem. A number of Hebrews from the Kingdom of Judah were taken captive by Babylonian forces. Among those taken was the above prophet Ezekiel. He was ordained and commissioned by God to be a prophet, a watchman, and teacher to the Ten Tribes of Israel who were held captive by Assyria. Assyria eventually was invaded by the Medes and driven north along with their Israelite captives.
Ezekiel's Flying Craft

While being held with other Jewish captives in Babylon, Ezekiel has described what we would today call a UFO experience. We can anticipate there will be scoffers and unbelievers at the mention of a flying craft, but carefully treat these words with the utmost sincerity as they are written in the Bible as part of Ezekiel's prophecy.

Many of today's Bible students and clergy are familiar with Ezekiel's description of the flying craft as reported in Ezekiel 1:1 & 8:1. He exhibits an amazing ability to describe in detail the workings and movements of something he had never before seen; what we would today call a UFO or a flying craft. He gives details of a flying object few of us have seen. He was 2500 years ahead of our time today. Many people around the world today have reported seeing similar craft; this has almost become a daily occurrence.

Apparently Ezekiel was a very observant and intelligent being. He had never seen a craft such as this; having observed only chariots or boats. He gives details of what we would call a mother ship in the sky with round windows all around the bottom of the craft and a crystal dome on the top. He describes the craft as being the color amber which was brasslike. Several smaller landing craft. were moving or hovering between the space craft and the earth with great speed. Ezekiel based his descriptions on only what he had seen or known in his lifetime.

Whether we choose to believe it, or not, this was a very specific depiction of a flying craft that carried people and several smaller landing craft! His description is not unlike descriptions of unidentified flying objects (UFOs) that folks claim they have seen in our own time! Other instances of flying craft are shown throughout the Bible. We know there will be those who will scoff and ridicule at the idea of Ezekiel seeing a real space ship, However, if you believe the bible to be true, you must believe what Ezekiel, a prophet, of God, reveals to us.

He received directions and commands from God who was on a throne inside the craft (Ezek 3:4):

"And he said unto me, Son of man, to, get thee unto the house of Israel, and Speak with my words unto them."

Although being part of the Jewish captivity, Ezekiel was to warn the members of the captive Ten Tribes, who were taken by the Assyrians in 721 B.C., He related events that are to take place during the latter days. These prophecies are meant for today's true Israel and definitely not the Jewish nation called Israel presently located in the middle east.

Who are Gog and Magog

This *latter day* Invasion of Israel will be led by northern forces known and identified in Ezekiel 38 & 39 as Gog and Ma'-gog. Strong's concordance identifies Gog and Ma-gog as a northern anti-Christian force:

From Strong's Exhaustive concordance

Gog *gogue* Symbolic name of a future anti-Christ
(Ma-gog essentially means the same)

From the description given Esau in Genesis 25, we can identify today's Russia as the descendents of Esau who was called Edom. From Genesis 25:29-30:

"And Jacob sod pottage: and Esau came from the field, and he *was* faint:

"And Esau said to Jacob, Feed me, I pray thee, with that same red *pottage*; for I am faint: Therefore was his name called Edom."

We see some symbolism here in that Esau ate the Red Pottage. And most of us recognize that Russia's national pottage is Borsch, which is red!

Many confederates, including the Arab states will join and be allied with them. Esau (or Edom) is today's Russia. The invading forces will be numbered in the ten's of millions and will assemble and come from the northern parts and cover the land as a cloud. Most Bible scholars and clergy are familiar with this prophecy; and they understand it to be an invasion by Russia and her confederates on today's Jewish nation called Israel located in the middle east. But they are mistaken. The invasion will be on America! The invasion likely will occur, possibly in the near future at a time identified as the *latter days* as indicated in Ezekiel 38:16:

"And thou shalt come up against my people of Israel, as a cloud to cover the land; it shall be in the *latter days*, and I will bring thee against my land that the heathen may know me, when I shall be sanctified in thee, O Gog, before their eyes."

Take note of the phrase; "as a cloud to cover the land." This seems to suggest that many aircraft, tanks, and other mechanized weapons of war, as well as a force we have never experienced will take part in this invasion. There also will be the modern day high tech computerized weapons of our time to include armor, missiles and special forces and millions of foot soldiers.

Note the significant phrase quoted in the above scripture; "that the heathen may know me." This is one of God's reasons for the invasion and the destruction of Russia's armies. Russia has always been a heathen unbelieving nation. After the destruction of 83 percent of Russia's armies, the heathen will definitely know Him!

Judah, Today's Israel in Palestine

The land called Israel in the middle east was formed in the year 1948 after the British Mandate expired. The land, from the time the Jews were returning early in the 1900's from Russia, Poland and Germany, was not known as Israel. The name *Israel* was an assumed name to identify the Jewish nation.

Believe it or not; the title *Israel* was never given to the Jews. Although they occupy the small nation in Palestine, they are not the Israel of which Ezekiel speaks.

The land more appropriately at the present time should be called Judea - home of the Jews. But it will be the future location of the Kingdom of God when Christ returns for the final advent.

The ancient land of Israel originally included all 12 tribes of Israel and included a vast area covering all of Palestine. The Jewish nation called Israel today covers only a small portion of Palestine and they are pulling back from some of these areas. The Gaza Strip has been evacuated at the time of this writing, but the land will greatly expand in size when the whole House of Israel is re-gathered into the land of Palestine. As the ancient prophets have stated; Israel will own and occupy all territory from the Nile to the Euphrates Rivers.

The re-gathering of Israel will include all Twelve Tribes of Israel; not just the Jews. Many of today's clergy have stated that the gathering has been completed. This is absolutely and emphatically not true. Not even the Jewish re-gathering has been completed. There are more Jews in America than there is in today's tiny Jewish state called Israel. The re-gathering of all of Israel has not even started yet!

Since 1948, Israel (or Judea), the home of the Jews, has been the target of aggression by the Arab states. We have seen many wars in the land as Arab neighbors have attacked the nation time and time again. No peace exists in the nation today. This nation is not at peace and dwelling safely as described in Ezekiel 38:11!

Fact is, this land does not meet any of the exacting specifications of true Israel that Ezekiel speaks of! Ezekiel's latter day Israel is not located anywhere in or near the middle east countries!

Today's Real Israel Defined

True latter day Israel is a land far away from Palestine and is located in a nation that is home to the people who rightly bear the title, *Israel.*

America is the land of Unwalled Villages.

The exact specifications of Ezekiel's Israel has been established and in his own words in Ezekiel 38:11 & 12 are as follows:
"And thou shall say, I will go up to the land of unwalled villages I will go to them that are at rest and dwell safely, all of them dwelling without walls and having neither bars nor gates..

"To take a spoil and to take a prey, to turn thine hand upon the desolate places that are now inhabited, and upon the people that are gathered out of the nations which have gotten cattle and goods, that dwell in the midst of the land."

Did you read that? Verse 11 mentions "unwalled villages."

It's obvious Ezekiel is NOT describing today's heavily walled Israel in the middle east because Ezekiel's Israel to be invaded must be a land of unwalled villages! The land known to the world with unwalled villages is America! Traditionally, this nation is a nation of immigrants and has no walls. Others are invited to our shores to escape harsh conditions and gain freedoms that are guaranteed to all men.

Israel in the middle east area is well known as a land of walled villages. The Jews have always had and are still building walls around their cities for protection from suicide bombers who want to enter their cities and murder citizens.

Theologians have puzzled over these characteristics of Ezekiel's Israel for decades. It's an enigma to them. It needn't be! Perhaps the descriptions of Israel have been subdued for a reason but are finally open for all to understand. Could it be we have finally been given the green light or keys to understanding today's prophecy?

A television prophecy teacher recently stated that the walls may not be standing at the time of the invasion; that Israel will have torn them down. This is his explanation of unwalled villages. He is wrong! Walls will always be part of today's tiny Israel.

There's a beautiful wall surrounding Jerusalem. This wall is of Biblical heritage and held sacred by Christians and Jews as well as Moslems. There is no way these cultures will allow the walls to be torn down.

Bars and gates are prominent leading into the cities to insure only those with proper identification and authority may enter. This is a security measure because of the danger to the citizens in the villages.

There are no walls and gates leading into American cities - the cities of Ezekiel's Israel.

Russia and her confederates want to take a spoil and to take a prey. They want to loot Israel of its riches including treasures, foods, technologies, cattle and other goods.

Today's Israel in Palestine is hardly the owner of such treasures. A raid on tiny Israel would hardly be worth the effort required by Russia, the largest nation on earth, and her allies and confederates. To invade this tiny nation once the spoils have been divided would be a waste.

Ezekiel describes true Israel as a desolate land that is now inhabited.

Ezekiel, in this part of the prophecy, is visualizing the land that Russia will invade. It is a land that once was desolate until the discovery by Columbus; and later many settlers came to the land. The land then became populated with people gathered out of the nations. It is a melting pot of different cultures from varied lands with a desire for freedom and opportunity; a land of large farms and ranches, orchards, minerals, riches, and general fatness of the land. It is a land of freedom, technology, commerce and industry. This is the land desired by Russia. They want the cattle and goods. Texas alone has an estimated 12 million plus head of cattle and other states across this great country have many more cattle.
.

Is Ezekiel describing America? The answer is an emphatic yes! Only America exactly fits the description of the Israel Ezekiel is describing. Most of the settlers of America are descended from one of the two major tribes of Israel and her descendents are today's modern Israel of the tribe of Manasseh; and the nation of Canada - which is also America are descended from Ephraim
Russia and her allies will invade America! Ezekiel has precisely described America as latter day Israel. No other country in existence today meets the specifications; only America. Neither has any nation in past history met these characteristics

of Israel as required by the prophecies of Genesis 49 describing the blessings to Joseph, the father of Ephraim and Manasseh. America and Canada are today's Manasseh and Ephraim. We are Israel!

Russian Invasion to Fail

The Russians will fail and her armies and armies of her confederates will be destroyed! This event could happen at any time. Don't be misled about what you have previously read and heard about this prophecy.

More than 83 percent of the invading forces will be destroyed including the Arab nations that participate in the raid and others who ally with Russia. Only a sixth part of Russia and her allies will survive the raid. Of course some Americans may also suffer as would be expected. We quote Ezekiel 29:2:

"And I will turn thee back, and leave but the sixth part of thee, and will cause thee to come up from the north parts, and I will bring thee upon mountains of Israel:"

Most clergy, bible students and teachers have completely and utterly misunderstood the conditions and characteristics of this prophecy as if they didn't exist.

We don't hesitate to repeat; the invasion will not be on today's small nation called Israel in the middle eastern area! The invasion will be on America!

Most of us are aware of the huge amount of preparation it took American and allied forces to invade Iraq. The staging and preparation was open for all to see. We watched the war effort develop on our big screen color television through nightly news programs. Such would be the case with Russia. There's no way they could secretly prepare an invasion involving their

14

armies and the armies of their confederates, the Arab nations, numbering in the millions without the whole world knowing it. Tiny Israel is surrounded by too many other small nations to afford Russia and her allies enough space to secretly stage such an invasion. And should the Jews detect such a build-up, they surely would break out the nuclear weapons and defend their nation.

Russia could hold maneuvers under the guise of joint military operations in eastern Siberia with her confederate Arab allies and others and secretly stage an invasion from there! There also are Russian submarines numbering in the hundreds scattered around the world and they are in constant maneuvering exercises.

Believe it folks. Russia will attempt a raid on America; not the tiny Israel in the land of Palestine! They have nothing to gain by invading tiny Israel.

The Jews were never given the title *Israel!* Although they, being descendants of Judah, which was one of the original tribes of Israel, will join the other members of the House of Israel when The Lord returns to set up His kingdom here on earth.

The Future of Israel

There are ten other tribes which are not yet inhabitants of today's nation called Israel in the Middle East! They dwell elsewhere and are very numerous; numbering in the hundreds of millions scattered throughout the nations. They are referred to as The Lost Tribes of Israel, and have not in any stretch of the imagination returned to Israel in the Middle East. Ezekiel in chapter 37:15-22 describes the final assembly of the House of Israel when the gathering takes place:

"The word of the Lord came again unto me, saying,

"Moreover, thou son of man, take thee one stick, and write upon it, For Ju'dah, and for the children of Israel his companions; then take another stick, and write upon it, For Joseph, the stick of E'phra-im, and for all the house of Israel his companions;

"And join them one to another into one stick; and they shall become one in thine hand.

"And when the children of thy people shall speak unto thee, saying, Wilt thou not shew us what thou *meanest* by these?
"Say unto them, Thus saith the Lord God; Behold, I will take the stick of Joseph which is in the hand of E'-phra-im, and the tribes of Israel his fellows, and will put them with him, *even* with the stick of Ju'dah, and make them one stick, and they shall be one in mine hand.

"and the sticks whereon thou writest shall be in thine hand before their eyes.

"And say unto them, thus saith the Lord God; Behold, I will take the children of Israel from among the heathen, whither they be gone, and will gather them on every side, and bring them into their own land:

"And I will make them one nation in the land upon the mountains of Israel; and one king shall be king to them all: and they shall be no more two nations, neither shall they be divided into two kingdoms any more at all:"

Today's middle eastern Israel has an estimated 6 million Jews; only a small fraction of the real House of Israel today. They have not yet achieved the re-gathering status described in the old testament prophecies.

Specifics of Israel Identified

16

From Ezekiel's specifications we review the identifying signs of true Israel:

- Must be a land of unwalled villages
- Must be at rest and dwelling safely
- Must not be a land of bars and gates
- Must have cattle and goods for a spoil and a prey
- Must be a land that was once desolate and is now settled

Ezekiel's prophecy of the Russian invasion has other descriptive elements that further pulls this prophecy away from the Middle East..

America and Russia have been enemies for decades. Soviet Russia's former premier, Nikita Khrushchev, once stated: "...we will bury you...!" Russia has desired and coveted America's riches, food, technology, minerals, cattle and other goods; and has been a threat of invasion since World War II. Actually, they have been a threat and a bully since biblical times!

We have fed them for decades with shipments of wheat and other goods from the vast breadbasket of America while they have wasted their time and effort developing various weapons and trying to outstrip the United States in Military prowess.

The Destruction of Russia

According to Ezekiel's prophecy, Russia and her allies will perish upon the mountains of Israel. Their carcass will be fed to the birds and beasts of the forest and fields.

"Thou shall fall upon the mountains of Israel, thou, and all thy bands, and the people that is with thee: I will give thee unto the ravenous birds of every sort and to the beasts of the field to be devoured." (Ezekiel 39:4)

Alaska, although not named, will likely figure into this prophecy as it is only fifty miles from the shores of Siberia:

"And I will turn thee back, and leave but the sixth part of thee, and I will cause thee to come up from the north parts, and I will bring thee upon the mountains of Israel..." (Ezekiel 39:2)

The prophecy also indicates divine intervention as told in Ezekiel 39:3:

"And I will smite thy bow out of thy left hand, and will cause thine arrows to fall out of the right hand."

Ezekiel 39:9 says it will take us seven years to clean up the carnage from the invasion:

"And they that dwell in the cities of Israel shall go forth, and shall set on fire and burn the weapons, both the shields and the bucklers, the bows and the arrows, and the handstaves, and the spears, and they shall burn them with fire for seven years."

Ezekiel has described the weapons of war of his own time; not knowing about today's modern warfare technology. Put into today's terms the above verse is stating that it will take us seven years to clean up and dispose of the carnage from the invasion.

A place will be reserved in Israel to bury Gog and her confederates (Ezekiel 39:11):

"And it shall come to pass in that day, that I will give unto Gog a place there of graves in Israel, the valley of the passengers on the east of the sea; and it shall stop the noses of the passengers and there shall they bury Gog and all his multitude; and they shall call it the valley of Ha'mon-Gog."

The location described above "east of the sea" could indicate a remote area in northwestern Alaska, east of the Bering Sea.

We will further show in the following chapters of this book overwhelming evidence that America is the subject Israel spoken of through this prophecy by Ezekiel!

Biblical Persia is Today's Iran

Ezekiel is describing the American continent as Russia's target. They have been planning this for decades. Today Russia and Iran are in cooperative patterns of creating atomic weaponry just for this purpose. If you look at the first few verses in Ezekiel 38, you will notice Persia is the first country mentioned in Russia's confederates to head this invasion attempt. The Biblical Persia is today's Iran! They have gone forward with their atomic energy development under the guise of creating atomic power plants for energy; yet they are one of the richest nations in the world in oil and they have no use for alternative "energy" as they claim. Their atomic energy program is hidden from the international inspectors. Iran has been importing weapons parts from other countries to include Russia, China and North Korea. Their proximity to Russia today makes it possible for them to send and receive any and all material and parts needed to succeed in the production of atomic weapons.

Iran has said they want to completely destroy today's Israel in the middle east. We must deal with a barbaric nation that has no reservations about neighboring states. Russia, the largest land mass nation in the world is pulling the strings of their soon to be allies.

CHAPTER TWO
More on the Tribes of Israel

In the preceding pages of this book, we have asserted that today's Israel in the Middle East is not the targeted Israel of Ezekiel 38 and 39. Ezekiel is really describing America!

You may ask how America became the real Israel; and we will present the facts that you may know that the Lost Tribes of Israel are scattered to many nations of the world. That one of the two Tribes holding the title *Israel* is indeed Great Britain, the descendants of Ephraim and the other tribe with the title Israel is America, the descendants of Manasseh. Again, we reaffirm the Jews (tribe of Judah) was never given the title Israel.

The Northern Ten Tribes are Invaded

At approximately 721 B.C. an invasion took place in the middle eastern land of Samaria. Millions of the inhabitants of that land were taken captive. The invasion, likely because of the massive number of people, took three years and was completed in 718 B.C. The invaders were the Assyrians. Those taken captive were the Ten Northern Tribes of Israel headquartered in Samaria. The Northern Tribes of Israel included Ephraim and Manasseh, joint holders of the birthright and title Israel; they were the most populous tribes of all Israel.

Most of the Israelite captives were taken into the Assyrian lands of Halah, Habor and Gozan, between the Euphrates and Tigris rivers, where they lived in slavery to the Assyrians for a while. The tribes of Reuben, Gad and the eastern half tribe of Manasseh likely were the first taken since they were located east of the Jordan river and were a smaller force that would have been easier to take than the nine and a half tribes who were in Samaria. Just why these three tribes were placed east of Jordan is not well explained in the bible, but we can assume they were placed there because of some racial and ethnic differences between the tribes. We will address this more fully in chapter 5 of this book.

Assyria was eventually invaded by the Medes and driven north, along with the Ten Tribes of Israel, into a mountainous region between the Caspian and the Black Seas and later across the Caucasus Mountains into an area known as Crimea. We in today's nations of America and Great Britain, for the most part, are Caucasians. We are descended from "those who crossed the Caucasus mountains" from which we get our racial designation.

The Tribes today are known as the Ten Lost Tribes of Israel. They are very prominent around the world and most of them don't realize just exactly who they are.

The Lost Tribes migrated into an area north of the Black Sea where they lived in exile. They remained in Crimean exile for many years and finally were dispersed or scattered to the East

21

and to the West. Although not commonly known, they are prominent in the lands of Europe and western lands of America and Australia and New Zealand as well as the British Isles; and to the countries of Asia. According to scriptures, the tribes were to be scattered to all nations East and West as well as North and South. They would go East and West and filter down into the south lands and some up to the north as well. Many of the descendants of Ephraim and Manasseh would be of the Anglo Saxon stock settling in the British Isles and on to America, Canada, Australia and New Zealand.

Seven Times Punishment

The Lost Tribes who carried and still carry the title, *Israel,* who were taken by the Assyrians in approximately 721 B.C., were warned in Deuteronomy 28 and Leviticus 26 that they would be punished seven times should they turn away from God. Israel lost their identity and never gained their great stature or blessings until the year 1800 (or there about). If we figure a year at 360 days and convert a day for a year, we find the time without God's blessings was 360 years times 7 times punishment would put them at 2520 years. And that is exactly what the curse by God entails. In today's math calculations:

1 year=360 days. calculated in Hebrew at that time. A year was 360 days Converting a day for a year = 360 years Seven times punishment: 7 x 350 years= 2520 years of punishment from 721 B.C.
The time of capture in Samaria.
360x7=2520 years   2520-721 B.C. = 1799 or 1800 AD

Israel gained back her favor from God in approximately 1800 A.D. At this time America gained much territory including the Louisiana Purchase which almost doubled their territories and became great, as was promised to Ephraim and Manasseh in Genesis 48:16. whose descendants still to this day hold the title, *Israel.*

God favored Israel as his chosen people early on; meaning He favored the nation and would offer the very best of everything. However, down through the ages Israel became defiant and very stubborn; a complaining lot. Israel was held captive for 400 years in Egypt as slaves doing all of their hard labor in building roads, buildings, etc. They were driven by the slave masters of Egypt. God heard their cry and preceded to free them from bondage with help from a reluctant Moses. Aaron, the brother of Moses, was the speaker for Israel when meeting with the Pharaoh. They saw first hand what miracles God could perform when sending the plagues upon Egypt. Moses was finally able to lead the Israelites out of slavery in Egypt under the protective hand of God.

Identification of the Ten Tribes of Israel

The Northern Ten Tribes of Israel originally were part of the whole House of Israel which included the following tribes named after the sons of Jacob:

Reuben	Zebulon	Asher	Issachar
Gad	Simeon	Levi	Judah
Joseph	Benjamin	Naphtali	Dan

The actual tribal count is thirteen tribes of Israel. The tribe of Joseph was split up into two tribes; the tribe of Ephraim and the tribe of Manasseh. Manasseh has the distinction of being the thirteenth tribe. Ephraim and Manasseh were two of the most populous of all the tribes. Many identify Manasseh, the thirteenth tribe, as America because of the symbols of our country including the 13 stripes on our flag and the number 13 represented in our official documents. If you look at the back side of a dollar bill, you will see 13 stars above the eagle, the eagle with an olive branch of 13 leaves, a shield with 13 stripes, a sheath of 13 arrows, 13 letters used in the word E Pluribus Unum as well as 13 letters in the words annuit coeptis over the pyramid, 13 stars in the chevron in the department of treasury emblem on the front, 13 courses in the pyramid on the left side. This is likely not a coincidence. Some think the British flag with the crossed bars represent the crossed arms of Jacob as he blessed the two sons of Joseph. You would naturally draw your own conclusions as this is not spelled out in the Bible.

A key to understanding the scriptures is knowing just which nations constitute today's true Israel as well as knowing the nation of Judah. Both nations are mentioned as two separate entities. Prophecies which involve both of these nations are shown throughout the Bible. Judah and Israel are still separate nations and will be until the time of the re-gathering by the Lord.

Following the reign of Solomon, the House of Israel was divided into two groups. The Northern Ten Tribes who resided in Samaria and were under the rule of Jeroboam. The Tribe of Judah (the Jews) was under the rule of Rheoboam in Jerusalem. The title, Jew, was merely a nickname for the Tribe of Judah.

At this time there were two separate Kingdoms: the Kingdom of Israel known as the Northern Ten Tribes of Israel headquartered in Samaria; and the Kingdom of Judah residing in Jerusalem. The tribe of Benjamin was included in the Kingdom of Judah. Benjamin was the smallest of all of the tribes as they were slain down to six hundred members by the other of the tribes of Israel because of a transgression as recorded in Judges 20.

Most Levites remained with the Tribe of Judah, although some were with the Northern Ten Tribes. The tribe of Levi had no inheritance and handled all affairs of the temples of Israel. The Northern Ten Tribes were in no way righteous. They had turned away from the commandments of the Lord and began idol worship. Jeroboam, who was the first king of the northern tribes replaced former priests with unqualified priests and they handled the affairs of the northern tribal worship activities by introducing pagan practices and idol worship.

The Northern Ten Tribes of Israel and the tribe of Judah were separated because of the sins of Solomon who had wives of the gentile nations that caused him to worship idols. We quote I Kings 11:11 thru 13:

"Wherefore the Lord said unto Solomon, Forasmuch as this is done of thee, and thou hast not kept my covenant and my statutes, which I have commanded thee, I will surely rend the kingdom from thee, and will give it to thy servant.

"Notwithstanding in thy days I will not do it for David thy father's sake; but will rend it out of the hand of thy son.

"Howbeit I will not rend away all the kingdom; but will give thee one tribe to thy son for David my servant's sake, and for Jerusalem's sake which I have chosen"

The Kingdom of Judah (the Jews) were taken captive by the Babylonians at 478 B.C. where they remained for seventy years. Cyrus, the king of Persia, was inspired by the Lord to allow the Jews to return and rebuild the temple and the kingdom of Judah. The Jews have since returned to Jerusalem and rebuilt the temple and the structures of the original ancient city. But, they have been overrun and scattered to the nations several times and are starting to return again to the small Jewish nation today called Israel. As we have discovered in chapter one, the Jews do not constitute the full House of Israel, but merely the Tribe of Judah. The Jews living in the little nation

25

of Israel today number less than six million; a small portion of Jews around the world today! The Ten Northern Tribes have not returned to their original homeland..

Unlike the times when the Ten Tribes of Israel were integrated within the whole House of Israel and included the tribe of Judah, they abandoned their covenant with the Lord and turned away from the commandments. They began idol worship and became evil and unidentified as to who they really were. They abandoned the Sabbath Day observance.

God established, and consecrated the seventh day of the week as the Sabbath Day. The Sabbath Day was to be a perpetual covenant throughout all generations. Israel was commanded to observe the true Sabbath for all time and eternity (Exodus 31:16-17):

"Wherefore the children of Israel shall keep the Sabbath, to observe the Sabbath throughout their generations, *for* a perpetual covenant.

"It is a sign between me and the children of Israel for ever; for *in* six days the lord made heaven and earth and on the seventh day he rested, and was refreshed."

When the Northern Ten Tribes lost this "sign", they lost their identity as belonging to Israel.

Because they broke the covenant with God, they were taken captive and eventually were scattered throughout the nations. Because they lost their identity, they became known as the Lost Tribes of Israel.

After the Ten Lost Tribes were driven from Assyria they migrated further north across the Caucasus Mountains. They became known as Caucasians because of their race. They then settled into the Crimean region north of the Black Sea where they lived in exile for many years. The tribes traveled east and traveled west settling into what is today's modern nations. The tribes did not vanish into thin air as some clergy and bible scholars would have you believe. There were numbered in the millions during their migrations and the time consumed in the migrations unto the final destination took hundreds of years.

Many clerics falsely claim the Lost Ten Tribes migrated only to Africa, India and other nations. We have seen programs on television attempting to trace the tribes to Africa, Ethiopia and India. Yet, most of them are right under our nose! There's no doubt that descendants of Israel can be found in all nations of the world, but the main scattering of the tribes were to the European, American and British nations.

Today's Nations of Israel

We can identify some of the nations that are inhabited by tribes of Israel.

Most Israelite racial traits are not unlike Adam from whom they descended; through Shem, Noah and the ancient fathers back to Adam. We quote from Strong's Concordance of Hebrew definitions:

Adam, aw-dam' to show blood in the face, i.e. *flush* or turn rosy:-be (dyed, made) red (ruddy)

Thus we are descendents of Israel and our ancestry goes all the way back to Adam. Some Israelites carry racial traits other than described above because of the racial intermingling over the years. We do not claim that to be of Israeli extraction, one must be white or Caucasian. As you will remember, Jacob made Joseph a *coat of many colors* while he was yet a child

27

and some believe, this to be a sign of identification to those of all races because Joseph was the father of Ephraim and Manasseh. As recorded in Genesis 41:35, Joseph was married to Asenath, an Egyptian woman which would introduce a different racial component into some of the descendants of Ephraim and Manasseh.

We can Identify some of the tribes of Israel this day as Denmark, Great Britain, Canada, America, Australia and New Zealand. Some have Identified Holland as descendants of Zebulon. Of course Denmark was the Tribe of Dan as the word Denmark is really *mark of Dan*. Dan also settled the kingdom of Ireland. Some of the tribe of Reuben was identified as France.

The larger part of the two son's of Joseph - Ephraim and Manasseh, - settled in the British Isles and were later separated as Great Britain explored and colonized around the world. Manasseh, through the Revolutionary War, became separated as was prophesied during the blessings by Jacob on Ephraim; "he also shall be great." Manasseh became today's America. This status holds true today as the British have maintained their land in the Isles of the Sea; the British Isles. They are the descendants of Ephraim. We are today's Israel! Remember the birthright as well as the title, *Israel* was given jointly to the two sons of Joseph by his father Jacob (Israel) while on his death bed. We quote from Genesis 48:16 as follows:

"...bless the lads; and let my name be named on them, and the name of my fathers Abraham and Isaac; and let them grow into a multitude in the midst of the earth."
(Israel's blessings on Ephraim and Manasseh)

While we, America and Great Britain, own the name Israel, we also are known by the name of Isaac: we are Isaac's sons or as shortened to the designation, Saxons. And better yet: Anglo

Saxons. Anglo is another name for England.

The name, British, is a Hebrew word meaning covenant man. The word Brit+=covenant and the word ish=man. Some letters are changed over the many years the tribes were on the move settling into different lands around the world.

And, as we are told in the scriptures, all gifts from God are without repentance. We quote Genesis 26:3

"...I will perform the oath which I sware unto Abraham..."

Find today's descendants of Manasseh and Ephraim and you have found true Israel!

The Scattering and Re-Gathering of Israel

Most prophets of the Old testament prophesied of the scattering of Israel and the re-gathering of the tribes. God will scatter the nation of Israel to all nations, but their location and identify will be known by God and none will be lost. Note: Israel will be scattered among *all* nations. So, we can expect to find the descendents of Israel in every nation on earth. They will be called again to return to their homeland in the Palestinian area.

Biblical Warnings and Promises

The House of Israel has been warned many times about turning right or left of the commandments of God. From the time Moses met with the Lord and gave the Ten Commandments unto this day, God has warned Israel about how to keep the laws and avoid the nature of the heathen. While traveling through the wilderness they were promised great rewards for obedience to God and obeying his commandments. Leviticus 26 and Deuteronomy 28 lists the promises God made to Israel if they would obey his commandments and put him first in their lives:

- The Lord promised the Children of Israel if they hearken to the voice of the Lord and obey all of his commandments he would set them high above nations on the earth. All these blessings would overtake them.

- They will be blessed in the cities as well as in the fields. The fruit of their body the fruit of the ground and the increase of their cattle will be blessed and increased. Their food basket and their stores will be blessed and increased. They will be blessed whether they are coming in or going out.

- Israel's enemies will be smitten before their face. They will come against thee one way and flee before thee seven ways. There will be blessings upon their store house and every thing they set their hands to.

- The Lord will establish His people as holy people unto himself.

- The people of the earth shall see them and know they are called by his name and be afraid of them. His people shall lend and not borrow. They shall become the head and not the tail. Israel shall not go aside from the Lord to worship idols.

- God has wonderful blessings for the Israelites that keep all his commandments and turn not aside. These blessings are available to the ones of us today who follow the commandments of God!

The Lord is showing the great blessings before showing the curses which will come upon Israel, should they depart from his commandments. God is, in this sense, a positive God. He doesn't want any of his children to receive punishment. As God has stated above; "...the earth shall see them and know they are called by his name." They are today's Christian nations (called by His name). All nations belonging to Israel are dotted with Christian Churches! So, although somewhat imperfect, most of the Christian Churches today belong to the nations of Israel. We are not gentiles. We are descendents of Israel and children of God!

But we must also be aware of the punishment God has promised would follow those who turn away from His Commandments and follow other gods.

"But it shall come to pass, if thou will not hearken unto the voice of the Lord thy God, to observe to do all His commandments and His statutes which I command thee this day; that all these curses shall come upon thee, and overtake thee." (Deuteronomy 28:15)

These curses are shown through Deuteronomy 28:15-68 what will happen should the children of Israel fail to obey God and follow his commandments. Following are some of the punishment to be upon Israel should they break their covenant and worship other gods:

- Cursed thalt thou be in the city, in the field, in thy breadbasket and thy store.
- Cursed shalt thou be in the fruit of thy body, the fruit of thy land and increase of kine.
- Cursed shalt thou be when thou comest in or go out.
- The Lord will send upon thee cursings, vexation, rebuke, in all thou try to do.
- Thou shalt be destroyed and perish because of thy wickedness in forsaking Me.
- The Lord will consume thee from off the land where

thy goest to possess it
- The Lord will smite thee with all manner of sickness.
- The heaven over thy head will become as brass and the ground as iron.
- The rain of the land will become as dust; thou will receive no rain.
- The Lord will cause thee to be smitten before thy enemies.
- Thy carcass will become meat for the birds and beasts of the earth.
- The Lord will smite thee with botch, emerods, scabs and itch.
- The Lord will smite thee with blindness, madness and astonishment of heart.
- Thou shall grope at midday as the blind gropeth. Thou shall not prosper in thy ways.
- Thou shall betroth a wife and another shall lay with her.
- Thou shall build a house and not dwell there in.
- Thou shall plant and another shall reap and eat of it.
- The ox shall be slain before thy eyes and thy enemy shall eat of it
- Thy sheep will be given to thy enemies.
- Thou will go mad with the sight of thine eyes because of what thou shall see.
- The enemy that thou knowest not shalt eat of the fruit of thy hand.
- Thou will be set before a king which shalt rule over thee.
- Thou shall become a slave to an unknown nation.

This is exactly what happened to the Northern Ten Tribes of Israel. They kept not his commandments when they set up idols to worship rather than going to Jerusalem for worship as was the practice before the separation. They feared Rheoboam, the king of Judah who had threatened them with hard labor and punishment.

Jeroboam set up golden calves in some of the cities of Samaria and moved the Sabbath day of worship. These practices remained with the Northern Ten Tribes through several reigns until the time of capture by the Assyrians.

We must always remember the Jews (tribe of Judah) was given the responsibility of ruler ship of all tribes of Israel:

"for Judah (Jews) prevailed above his brethren, and of him came the chief ruler; but the birthright was Joseph's." (1 Chronicles 5:2)

The birthright was given to Joseph's two sons -Ephraim and Manasseh - and included the title *Israel*. We are today's Israel that Ezekiel speaks about in Ezek 38 & 39.

Jews and Gentiles

Many in the Christian movements today do not know the differences between Jew and gentile. Today's clergy think all that are not Jews are surely gentiles. This is not biblical and we will explore the gentile vs Jew controversy.

A gentile throughout the Old Testament is anyone who does not belong to or is not descended from the tribes of Israel. The Jews are one, and only one, of the tribes of Israel. There are eleven more tribes. If you are descended from Reuben, Gad or Benjamin, or any tribe of Israel, you are not a gentile. You do not have to be a Jew!

The first biblical usage of the word, gentile, was in Genesis 10:5 just after the genealogy of Japheth describing his sons who ventured into their nations with their own language after their families. They were called the isles of the Gentiles.

The nation of Judah (Jews) had not been established at this

time. Judah was not even born. So, Japheth stood alone as the only gentiles mentioned in the bible at this time.

Webster's Collegiate Dictionary defines a gentile as:

Gen'tile (jen'til) 1, (Bible) a person not a Jew 2. in respect to any religious group, an outsider.

It is commonly known there are religious organizations that consider those other than their own membership as gentiles. In that respect, Webster is right in his second part of the description. However, we know from previous words of the bible and this book that there are twelve tribes of Israel (of which Judah, the Jews, are one) who are not gentiles. All the way through the Old Testament the reference is made between Israelites and gentiles - not Jews and gentiles. There were no Jews, known by that name, until long after the Twelve Tribes of Israel were in Canaan. In this respect, Webster is wrong in his definition of gentiles.

No Tribes of Israel nor their descendents are gentiles.

There are in existence descendents of the Ten Tribes of Israel dwelling in various locations on earth at this time and in very large populations that were descended from the original House of Israel that are not gentiles. Israelites likely are today's Christian nations of the world. Webster's first definition more correctly should read:

Gen'tile 1. (Bible) a person not an Israelite.

Today's clergy have a rough time separating the tribe of Judah (Jews) from the remaining tribes of Israel. The Jews is merely a nickname to describe the tribe of Judah. The word, Jew, first appeared in II Kings 16:6, at which point the tribe of Judah was at war with the northern Ten Tribes of Israel and their allies. Following this classification the Jews became a byword to describe Israel. However, they do not represent the real nation of Israel, but only the tribe of Judah; the Jews. As we have said in the above writings, the full Twelve Tribes of Israel will be gathered at the time of the second advent of Jesus Christ to earth to set up the twelve tribed House of Israel which will become the Kingdom of God with Christ in Jerusalem as the head!

CHAPTER Three
The British Commonwealth of Nations

The descendents of Ephraim, known today as Great Britain, colonized almost 60 nations around the globe. This was fulfillment of a prophecy made by Jacob during his blessings on the two sons of Joseph as shown in Genesis 48:17-19:

"And when Joseph saw that his father laid his right hand upon the head of Ephraim, it displeased him: and he held up his father's hand, to remove it From Ephraim's head unto Manasseh's.

"And Joseph said unto his father, not so, my father: for this is the firstborn; put thy right hand upon his head.

"And his father refused, and said, I know *it*, my son, I know *it:* he also shall become a people, and he also shall be great: but truly his younger brother shall be greater than he, and his seed shall become a multitude of nations."

Jacob, the patriarch of Israel, placed his right hand upon the head of Ephraim and his left hand upon the head of Manasseh which required him to cross his arms. Normally, the right hand would be upon the head of the older brother indicating the greater blessing, but because of some differences in the role they would play in the end, Ephraim received the greater blessing.

And we know the descendents of Ephraim did grow into a multitude of nations; or as we would say; *A Commonwealth of Nations*. The commonwealth of nations is still in existence today although not as prominent as they were in the last 200 years.

The British Commonwealth of Nations brought order to most of the world through their colonization of many countries. America was a British colony until they broke from England during the Revolutionary War and formed their own government as was promised in the above scripture; "...he also shall become a nation...." America is today's descendents of Manasseh, who received the lesser blessing from Jacob. Having jointly received the blessings of the birthright, Great Britain and America are today's Israel. These blessings for the latter days were shown in Genesis 48:16:

"The angel which redeemed me from all evil, bless the lads; and let my name Be named on them, and the name of my fathers Abraham and Isaac; and let Them grow into a multitude in the midst of the earth."

We have spoken of the half tribes of Manasseh with a half tribe located east of the Jordan river and the western half tribe located in Samaria, west of the Jordan river. The tribes were apparently split because of their final destiny or where their final habitation would be. The Bible indicates there are splits in

37

other tribes as well.

The Tribe of Dan was split and at the time of the Assyrian siege, portions of Dan were taken with the other tribes into Assyrian captivity. Part of the Tribe of Dan were seafarers and at the siege, they fled in their ships to today's countries of Spain and Portugal or the Iberian Peninsula as was prophesied by Moses in Deuteronomy 33:22:

"And of Dan he said, Dan is a lion's whelp; he shall leap from Ba'-shan.

Many believe "leap from Bashan" is actually escaping before the Assyrian siege. It is believed the siege started east of the Jordan River where Bashan was under the half tribe of Manasseh who had the leadership and constituted part of the territories east of Jordan.

Jeremiah and Tribe of Dan Settle Ireland

Those of the Tribe of Dan who were seafarers eventually went on to the island nation of Ireland off England's western shores. Irish history and some legends tell of the settling of Ireland by the Tribe of Dan. A prophet named Jeremiah was instrumental in settling this country. Ezekiel prophesied of the changes that would be made in the transfer of royalty from Jerusalem to a high mountain which we would identify today as the British Isles; to include Great Britain, Scotland and Ireland.

Jeremiah was ordained a prophet by the Lord before he was born and as told in Jeremiah, he was assigned the chore of overseeing the destruction of Jerusalem (Jeremiah 1:4-10):

"Then the word of the Lord came unto me, saying, "Before I formed thee in the belly, I knew thee; and before thou camest forth out of the womb I sanctified thee, and I ordained thee a prophet unto the nations.

"Then said I, Ah, Lord God! behold, I cannot speak; for I *am* a child.

"But the Lord said unto me, Say not, I *am* a child: for thou shall go to all that I shall send thee, and whatsoever I command thee thou shalt speak.

"Be not afraid of their faces; for I *am* with thee, to deliver thee, saith the Lord.

"Then the Lord put forth his hand, and touched my mouth. And the Lord Said unto me, Behold, I have put my words into thy mouth.

"See, I have this day set thee over the nations and over the kingdoms, to root out, and to pull down, and to destroy, and to throw down, to build, and to plant."

The last part of the above scripture (verse 10) is summarizing that Jeremiah will oversee the destruction of the Kingdom of Judah in Palestine and will "build and plant" the kingdom elsewhere. He was to see to the three part movement of the kingship of Judah after the siege of Babylon. According to Ezekiel, the crown would thrice be moved (Ezek. 21:27):

"And thou profane wicked prince of Israel, whose day is come, when iniquity *shall have* an end,

"Thus saith the Lord God; Remove the diadem, and take off the crown: this *shall* not be the same: exalt *him that is* low, and abase *him that is* high.

"I will overturn, overturn, overturn, it; and it shall be no *more*, until he come whose right it is; and I shall give it *him*."

Three overturns was the transfer of the kingship from Jerusalem to Ireland, Scotland and finally to Great Britain where the kingship would finally be established.

The tribe of Judah was of the royalty line of Israel. All kings (and queens) of Israel would be descendants of Judah.(Gen 49):

"The sceptre shall not depart from Judah, nor a lawgiver from between his feet, until Shiloh come; and unto him shall the gathering of the people be."

This was a dual blessing on Judah given by Jacob shortly before his death. A descendant of the tribe of Judah would always reign over Israel until the return of Shiloh (Jesus Christ) to set up his kingdom on earth. The second part of the blessing was that wherever the kingdom of Judah was located in the last days, this also would be the gathering place of the Twelve Tribes of Israel. And as we know, the kingship still remains in England today, ruling over Israel, but the tribe of Judah is located in Palestine and carry the name of their future kingdom; Israel.

The last king, Zedekiah, was a descendent of a long line of kings from Pharez, one of the twin sons of Judah. The prophecy states Zedekiah would be taken captive by the Babylonians and eventually blinded and killed and we know from scripture this was so.

The kingship line of Pharez would no longer rule in Jerusalem. Jerusalem would be destroyed. The royal house then would be ruled over by a descendant of the line of Zara. Which fulfills the prophecy, "exalt *him that is* low, abase *him that is* high," meaning raise the line of Zara into the kingship of Judah and take away the line of Pharez. A daughter of Zedekiah named Tea Tephi, was wedded to a descendant of Zara, King Eochaidh II, and their descendents still reign as today's monarchy of Great Britain.

Numerous artifacts were brought to Ireland by Jeremiah, including David's harp, which became the national symbol of Ireland and still holds true today. The harp is shown on the flag of Ireland as well as other prominent areas within the government. The harp is also shown on commercial products of Ireland. Jeremiah also brought with him his scribe, Baruch, and the daughters of Zedekiah as well as other artifacts. According to legend and Irish history, Jeremiah was instrumental in setting up the government of Ireland and is buried there near the ancient government seat of Tara.

Judah Rules Israel

The birth of Pharez and Zara was the result of a relationship between Judah and Tamar, the daughter in law of Judah (Gen. 38:11- 18):

"Then said Judah to Tamar his daughter in law, Remain a widow at thy father's house, till She'-lah my son be grown: for he said, Lest peradventure he die also, as his brethren *did*. And Tamar went in her father's house.

"And in process of time the daughter of Shuah Judah's wife died; and Judah was comforted and went up unto his sheepshearers to Timnath, he and his friend Hirah the A-dul'-lamite.

"And it was told Tamar, saying, Behold thy father in law goeth up to Timnath to shear his sheep.

"And she put her widow's garments off from her, and covered her with a veil, and wrapped herself, and sat in an open place, which *is* by the way to Timnath; for she saw that She'-lah was grown, and she was not given unto him to wife.

"When Judah saw her, he thought her *to be* an harlot; because she had covered her face.

"And he turned unto her by the way, and said, Go to, I pray thee, let me come into thee; (for he knew not that she *was* his daughter in law.) And she said, What wilt thou give me, that thou mayest come in unto me?

"And he said, I will send *thee* a kid from the flock. And she said, Wilt thou give *me* a pledge, till thou send *it?*

"And he said, What pledge shall I give thee? And she said, Thy signet, and thy bracelets, and thy staff that *is* in thine hand. And he gave *it* her, and came in unto her, and she conceived by him."

Tamar eventually gave birth to twins and named them Pharez and Zara. Pharez, being the firstborn, was given the royalty line and would be the father of all of the kings of Israel.

This changed after the destruction of Jerusalem and the royal house and the captivity of the tribe of Judah. The overturn of the Throne of Israel today gives Great Britain royalty the title of the King of Israel. Thus, the monarchy of England is descended from Judah!

Jacob's Pillar Stone

The coronation of British Royalty has a unique history. Do the Brits realize they are being ruled over by a descendent of Judah? The throne upon which all kings and queens of England have been coronated sits at Westminster Abbey in London. It is a very unique piece of furniture although very rustic. The throne is made of wood and has a compartment across the bottom which holds a stone called by several names; Liafail, Stone of Scone and the Stone of Destiny. The sign next to the stone calls it Jacob's Pillar Stone. Supposedly, it is the same stone Jacob anointed in Luz during his journey from Padana-ram (Gen. 35:11-15):

"And God said unto him, I *am* God Almighty: be fruitful and multiply; a nation And a company of nations shall be of thee, and kings shall come out of thy loins.

"And the land which I gave Abraham and Isaac, to thee I will give it, and to thy Seed after thee will I give the land.

"And God went up from him in the place where he talked with him.

"And Jacob set up a pillar in the place where he talked with him, *even* a pillar Of stone: and he poured a drink offering thereon, and he poured oil thereon.

"And Jacob called the name of the place where God spake with him, Beth-el."

It is believed this stone is the very same stone that is seen in the compartment under the throne where all English royalty have been coronated. The Brits have a close tie to the history of Ireland and Scotland where the Stone has been previously located. The three overturns spoken by Ezekiel is the three locations where the stone was present. Legends and poems have described the saga of the stone of Scone, or Jacob's Pillar Stone and the Hebrew name of the stone, Liafail. Geological examinations show the stone to be of the same composition as stones found in the biblical area of Bethel. The name Bethel literally means House of God. It is believed by many that where the stone is found, there will be the presence of God.

The Israelites carried this stone with them in all their travels since leaving Egyptian captivity and was used in coronation of all kings of Israel. Moses used the stone to furnish water during travel of the Israelites through the Sinai wilderness.

CHAPTER Four
Half Tribe of Manasseh

Before the House of Israel settled in Canaan the land to be taken and possessed was apportioned by Moses and carried out by Joshua. There were two divisions after the whole house of Israel battled with the Canaanites to assume their land. The largest division was west of the river Jordan while the smaller division was east.

We have heard and read a lot about the half Tribe of Manasseh. The bible is not explicit as to why there is a "half" tribe. The half tribe most prominent in the Bible is the eastern half tribe beyond Jordan. There naturally would be another half tribe of Manasseh which is identified in the Bible as the western half tribe. When land was apportioned, Moses assigned a portion of territory east of Jordan to one of the Half Tribes of Manasseh for an inheritance. Also parts of this area was assigned to the Tribe of Gad and the Tribe of Reuben (Joshua 13:29-32.):

"And the border of the children of Reuben was Jordan, and the border *thereof.* This was the inheritance of the children of Reuben after their families, the cities and the villages thereof.

"And Moses gave inheritance unto the tribe of Gad, even unto the children of Gad according to their families.

"And Moses gave *inheritance* unto the half tribe of Man-nas'seh: and *this* was *the possession* of the half tribe of the children of Ma-nas'seh by their families.

"And their coast was from Ma-ha-na'im, all Ba'shan, all the kingdom of Og king of Ba'shan, and all the towns of Ja'ir which *are* in Ba'shan, threescore cities:

"And half Gilead, and Ash'ta-roth, and Ed're-i, cities of the kingdom of Og in Ba' in Ba'shan, *were pertaining* unto the children of Ma'chir the son of Ma-nas'seh, *even* to the one half of the children of Ma'chir by their families.

We know the western half tribe of Manasseh remained in Canaan with the balance of the house of Israel.

Some of the Levitical priesthood were present in the tribes east of the Jordan as well as being prominent in the western tribes. Levi and Simeon were to be divided into all tribes of Israel (as explained in Gen. 49: 5 & 7:

"Simeon and Levi *are* brethren, instruments of cruelty *are in* their habitations.

"Cursed be their anger, for it was fierce; and their wrath, for it was cruel: I will Divide them in Jacob, and scatter them in Israel."
So, we see elements of other tribes were scattered in the eastern division of Israel. The tribe of Levi maintained temple af-

fairs in their travels with the main division of Israel as well as a presence within the eastern tribes.

Why East of Jordan

Was there something significant about the eastern half tribe of Manasseh. Were they, along with Gad and Ruben, given their inheritance east of Jordan for a reason? Was there a racial or ethnic difference? Were they being separated for a specific purpose? All cultures and populations have had groups that didn't fit in with the main group. Could it be the eastern Half tribe of Manasseh with Reuben and Gad were the renegade tribes from the "other" side of the tracks (or in this case, the other side of the river). Did they not fit in socially with the elite tribes of Canaan? We know there was strife within the tribes and more so between Ephraim and Manasseh.

The eastern half tribe was to be separated from the western tribes only after they helped take the western area of Canaan for the nine and a half tribes of the west. It seems the likely reason was because of their personal traits; that they possessed a warrior characteristic that would allow them to perform a specific role. We can only speculate that some of these tribes of the east were placed there as a prearrangement to a future movement to the far eastern countries where they would in part be scattered.

As we search the ancestry of these tribes we find Joseph, the father of Manasseh, was descended from Rachael by Jacob. Reuben was the firstborn of Israel through Leah, the sister to Rachael. Reuben was not given the birthright of Israel because he defiled his father's bed, having had an affair with Bilhah, Rachael's handmaiden. And Gad was descended from Zilpah by Jacob.

Because of their isolation from the main body of Israel, the tribes east of Jordan likely were taken first by the Assyrian forces at the time of the scattering of Israel. They were driven north across the Caucuses Mountains and into exile in the Crimean region north of the Black Sea. From there some would eventually reach eastern Asia through China, Manchuria, Korea and further to Japan. They were likely the Ainu who originally settled in northeastern Japan. At one time the British liked to think of Japan as Great Britain of the Atlantic. Japan exhibits many of the traits of modern day Manasseh which we will discuss later. They likely settled there and have been there until the present time.

Israel in Asia

It becomes apparent God has spread the Ten Tribes of Israel to the four corners of the earth to include the far eastern areas of Asia as recorded Gen 28:12-14:

"And he dreamed, and behold a ladder set up on the earth and the top of it reached to heaven and behold the angels of God ascending and descending on it.

"And behold, the Lord stood above it, and said, I am the Lord God of Abraham thy father, and the God of Isaac: the land whereon thou liest, to thee will I give it, and to thy seed.

"And thy seed shall be as the dust of the earth, and thou shall spread abroad to the west, and to the east, and to the north, and to the south: and in thee and in thy seed shall the families of the earth be blessed."

During the spreading of Israel from the Crimean region all did not all go west, but some went east to the far eastern countries to include Japan.

Jeroboam, of the tribe of Ephraim, became the king of the Northern Ten Tribes of Israel after the separation from the tribes of Judah and Benjamin. Since Ephraim and Manasseh were given the co-title *Israel*, if follows that the leadership role would be confirmed in Jeroboam. As you may recall, Ephraim received the greater blessing (Genesis 48:19).

In the absence of Ephraim, Manasseh would normally take the lead. Proper leadership was necessary in the allocation of land east of Jordan. Ma'Chir of the half Tribe of Manasseh became the leader of the eastern tribes which included Reuben, Gad and a handful of others. When we speak of the tribes of Reuben, Gad and half tribe of Manasseh, we are referring to the descendants of the tribes who maintained tribal status and lived within their own tribal arrangements; most married within their tribes. The population count of all Israel at the time was in the millions.

If the "eastern" half tribe was scattered to eastern Asia after their period of exile in the Crimean region, it was likely they were more compatible with their neighbors, Gad and Reuben, who went east with them, although some went with the main migration through western Europe. There likely was nobody at the time ordering them to go hither or yon. They, in all probability, decided to go east to escape harsh treatment from the other tribes. This was a move that they were compelled to make without too much reasoning in order to fulfill prophecy; that Israel would scatter to the east and west and to all nations.

We can surmise there exists today the descendents of these tribes in the territory we refer to as the Far East and Japan. We could then assume there are presently two tribes of Manasseh which would be the Anglo-Saxon Tribe of Manasseh in America and the Far Eastern Tribe of Manasseh living in the Asian Island countries today of Japan and possibly some in Korea. Both Japan and South Korea are allied defense and trading partners with America and are head and shoulders above their neighboring countries in social order, commerce, and technological ability. That Japan is descended from Israel is not conclusive, although some artifacts and writing of historians suggest so.

Far Eastern Artifacts

There are astounding comparisons between the Israelites and the nation of Japan, both in their culture and religious customs.. Bible historians and researchers have identified artifacts found in the Crimea, i.e., Hebrew epitaphs found in cemeteries north of the Black Sea, which is south of Russia, and identified as ancient Scythia.

Parts of Israel lived there in exile as the start of the scattering. They occupied the whole of Crimea and held it. They lived there, died there and were buried there. Some had epitaphs on their tombs. Researchers have discovered these tombs and one shows the epitaph of a man who was of the tribe of Reuben. It states that the territory had been occupied by Gad, Reuben and the half tribe of Manasseh. This shows these three tribes east of the Jordan river had remained together in the Crimea territory. After being scattered to that vicinity for a long period of time they finally migrated east toward Mongolia, China and Korea and finally to the Isles of Japan in far eastern Asia. Korea was also given the name Chosen. Could this be a reminder that some of the people that passed through this land are descended from God's "chosen" people? And we know there is today a separation between the north and south of Korea.

When the tribes were on the move westward, Ephraim, the holder of the greater blessing, was still the leader of all tribes. Manasseh, the other holder of the title, Israel, still would maintain the leadership role in the absence of Ephraim. Thus, the migration east toward Japan was under the lead of Manasseh.

The epitaph stated that a portion of the tribe of Manasseh along with Gad and Reuben had moved away east as far as China and beyond. God said, through his prophets, that He would scatter Israel east and west to all nations (Gen.23:14). There's more evidence that they were scattered as far as Japan and formed the nation there.

The Japanese are racially and culturally different from the Chinese and other Asian inhabitants living in that part of the world. The Japanese are light brown when compared to the other Asians who are traditionally of the yellow or mongoloid race. The western world has questioned where they came from and nobody seems to know for sure.

Japan was a country divided up among a number of clans presided over by an emperor traced back to the Sun Goddess. Traditionally the Sun goddess in Egypt was none other than Asenath who married Joseph the son of Jacob. Japanese historical traditions say they came from the far west of Asia approximately 2500 years ago. This would put the arrival in Japan just after the time of the scattering of Israel. If this rings true, they could be traced all the way back to the vicinity where the above epitaphs were found, in the Crimean region, and further on to the middle east.

According to Genesis 41:46, Joseph married the daughter of Potiphar, a dark skinned Egyptian woman, named Asenath who became the mother of Ephraim and Manasseh. Being directly descended from Adam whose complexion was described as "ruddy," Joseph, the father of Ephraim and Manasseh, would be of the same characteristic as the white Caucasians of today. When Egyptians marry Caucasians, their offspring sometimes resemble the characteristics of today's Japanese. World history says Japan was of Mongoloid stock although some Caucasoid is present which is difficult to account for. These, called the Ainus, were at the beginning of the historical era, mainly to be found in the northeastern parts of the Japanese Islands including Hokkaido. So, we have a connection although it not conclusive that the Japanese are today's far eastern Manasseh.

From the beginning of the historical era down to the present day, the keys to the continuity of Japan as a society have been the family.

The clan (tribe) was an enlarged family, and the nation was the most enlarged family of all. In patriarchal style, the emperor presided over the national family as tribal leader would preside over the clan - or even the small farmer over his family. This closely resembles the original organization of the House of Israel.

Some of the tools and methods of agriculture are about the same as used by the Israelites. There are many similarities in their customs, religion, and habits seen in Japan today. Some of Japan's traditions sprang from far western Asia. Also some of their musical instruments were similar.

Investigating the characteristics of Japanese worship we find similarities to Israeli worship.

Shintoism is the religion of Japan as opposed to Buddhism found in most of Asia. They are unlike. There is some Buddha worship in Japan that was imposed on them. Buddha worship includes idol worship. There are no Idols in Shinto temples.

One of Japan's religious practices is reminiscent of the crossing of the river Jordan by the Israelites when they first came to the land of Canaan. Japanese priests would take a box from the temple and carry it down to a body of water and wade out into the water, turn and go back taking the box back into the temple. This custom is carried on periodically and has been a custom for centuries. Nobody there can remember how it got started and why. There are more customs relating to the practices of the Israelites. The priestly dress is similar to the Levitical temple dress.

Samurai or Samaria Warriors?

The tribes of Gad, Reuben and the half tribe of Manasseh were allowed to assume their inheritance east of Jordan only after the Canaanites were defeated in the west. They were taken with the other tribes of Israel into Canaan to battle for the inheritance of the other tribes there. The nine and a half tribes of Israel apparently were incapable of earning their territory and had to have the eastern tribes to help win the territories. There's no mention of the western tribes returning the favor. The eastern tribes of Gad, Reuben and half tribe of Manasseh apparently were good warriors. During the tribal blessings of Genesis 49:19, Gad was told he would be an over comer:

"Gad, a troop shall overcome him: but he shall overcome at the last."

One wonders if this is where the Sumurai warriors originated that were so prominent in Japan. Could Samurai be a corruption of the word, Samaria the former home of the Ten Tribes of Israel: Samurai Warriors = Samaria Warriors ?

There are other similar characteristics such as the word Saki, a common word used in the names in Japan. Saki is short for Isaac; with the "I" dropped from the first part of that name, and other characters added or removed, i.e., the city of Osaka and Nagasaki. Their national drink, a Japanese wine, is pronounced "saki."

Before we get too far ahead in trying to connect Japan to Manasseh, lets compare the similarities to the promises in Genesis

49: 22-26 to the state of the Japanese nation today:

Manasseh was to became a very prominent nation in the affairs of the world. Today's America has attained and even surpassed the prophetic promises made to Ephraim and Manasseh. They were to reap the "fat of the land" and to have increase in the womb (many offspring) and to reap the riches of the deep and things that lie beneath the earth including the vast farmland and minerals from the earth. They were to occupy many lands and control the gates of their enemies.

Far Eastern Prominence

Japan, likewise, was well recognized in that they, a much smaller country, have occupied China, Korea and   other nations. They became a fighting force and attacked the United States, at Pearl Harbor which caused America to enter World War II. Japan failed in the effort losing out to the United States. But still it proved Japan was a well organized military power.

As was promised to Ephraim and Manasseh that they would control the gates of their enemies, Japan also controlled the gates of their enemies in the Asian areas.

Japan has reaped the fruit of the earth and of the deep as was promised to Manasseh. They have enjoyed the harvests of the seas surrounding the nation. They live on their huge rice and grain harvests. They have outdone all other nations in Asia with their industries. The manufacture and sale of electronic devices for domestic and industrial use has outstripped and overwhelmed other Asian market nations. Japan has a proud history of everything they have undertaken. They are totally unlike other East Asian nations.

Japan has entered the space program as they are the premier space power in Asia. Japanese astronauts have gone into space

5 times with American space travelers - the most recent one, Soichi Noguchi, going to the space station in July of 2005. Noguchi is from the city of Chigasaki (there's that name again - saki).

The United States has purchased more automotive, agricultural, earth moving and road building machines from Japan than any other offshore industrial nations. We have made them super wealthy with our purchase of cars, motor cycles, and other recreational vehicles and electronics goods as well as reconstruction of their nation after the war.

Japan, like the United States of America, is a world leader in manufacturing, economy and finance. They launched their first ship for commercial purposes in 1951 and later became the largest shipyard in the world! By 1970 Japan's GDP was the second greatest in the non-communist world, and by the end of the 1980's, they were the world's second largest economic power in terms of GDP. They have defense protection from the Americans - their other Manasseh!

Japan is prominent as a nation in the world society. They along with such nations as Great Britain, America, France and Russia sit on the Security Council of the United Nations. They are a people with a proud achievement history in all things!

So, we see Japanese astronauts going to the space station via the American space shuttles. It becomes obvious they are eager to take a lead in international affairs.

As we can surmise, Japan far exceeds the technological, cultural and social development of neighboring nations.

Many believe, because of the prominence of Japan and

their successes, their might and the fact they came into existence 2500 years ago, they likely are descended from the Tribes of Israel. We must remember the Tribes of Israel were promised to spread to the four corners of the earth.

CHAPTER Five
End Time Israel

Earlier on we talked about end time Israel and the fact that today's whole House of Israel does not occupy Palestine in the Middle East at this time except for part of the Tribe of Judah (the Jews). Judah is one tribe - and only one tribe - of the house of Israel. There are no descendants of Dan, Ephraim, Manasseh or other tribes in the small country called Israel today. However, there are descendants of all of the tribes of Israel scattered around the world. Today they are known as the Lost Tribes of Israel. They, for the most part, do not even know who they are at this time. The Lost Tribes of Israel are very massive. It would be difficult for the whole area of Palestine to contain the total number of the tribes of Israel living around the world today. The whole House of Israel living today are called the remnant of Israel throughout the bible. And they would be a remnant of the number promised to Rebecca - thousands of millions!

The population of today's Israel in the Middle East is only 6 million and part of the inhabitants there are of Palestinian and other races. The actual estimated population of Jews living there is less than 6 million; hardly the massive population of the sands of the seashore nor as the stars in the sky as promised Abraham, Isaac and Jacob and their descendants. The Jewish population would swell immensely should all the tribe of Judah (Jews) return to their homeland today. They could not contain the additional Ten Lost Tribes. The land area will be reapportioned as outlined in Ezekiel 48:1-35 to include a large area for each tribe of Israel numbering in the millions.

Christ will gather the Lost Ten Tribes from around the world back to their ancient homeland in Palestine at the second advent. They will join with the Tribes of Judah (the Jews) and Benjamin to restore the original House of Israel as it was in the days of David and Solomon. Jesus Christ will reign as King of Kings over the whole house of Israel as well as the world. This will be the final gathering and will be initially for a thousand year reign and then forever.

Prophecy dealing with Israel in the *Latter Days* is told throughout the Bible. A lot of today's clergy focus their attention on events of the New Testament and completely ignore the Old Testament. Much latter day prophecy found in the Old Testament reveals what is to happen in the end times.

Having knowledge about end times or latter day prophecy should not change your beliefs in whatever church you attend; as the objective of any Bible based church should be to increase knowledge to all members. It will open up more understanding regarding the events in the world that are taking place at this time.

Many prophetic promises were made by our forerunners that concerns all of us in the present day and age. Most clergy, Bible teachers and students believe we are living in the last days. When prophecies are made, a time or indication of when the prophesied event will take place is usually revealed.

Early Promises

A prophecy that Abraham's descendants would be as numerous as the sands of the sea shore or the stars in the sky is shown in Genesis 22:17 & 18:

"That in blessing I will bless thee, and in multiplying, I will multiply thy seed as the stars in the heaven, and as the sand which *is* upon the sea shore; and thy seed shall possess the gate of his enemies.

"And in thy seed shall all the nations of the earth be blessed; because thou hast obeyed my voice."

God goes on to reaffirm these promises to Isaac which were made unconditional to Abraham as told in Genesis 26:3:

"Sojourn in this land, and I will be with thee, and will bless thee; for unto thee and unto thy seed, I will give all these countries, and I will perform the oath which I sware unto Abraham thy father."

And so, the repetition of this promise made to Abraham and now being made to Isaac will be repeated to Rebekah and on to Jacob and his descendants.

These prophecies are not just idle promises to complete a volume of works, but are an ongoing promise that is coming true and will continue until fulfillment. This is a three fold prophecy as follows:

- Thy seed will be numerous as the stars in the sky and

the sands of the sea shore.
- Thy seed shall possess the gate of his enemies.
- In thy seed shall all nations of the earth be blessed.

God through a very select group of descendants of Abraham, Isaac and Jacob has performed much of this prophecy. The words that say; "I will multiply thy seed as the stars of the heaven, and as the sands which is upon the sea shore" has been almost completed in the Tribes of Israel. The count over the years up through today is very numerous and as the sands of the seashore. We are still growing! Israel is tribally represented throughout almost all of the world in the hundreds of millions.

Most inhabitants of Christian nations are descendants of the tribes of Israel.

Israel was to control the waterways and oceans of the world as well as land gates.

Great Britain and the United States have indeed controlled the gates of their enemies with control of the sea lanes, the canal gates of the waterways of the world and the passages from country to country including control of the Panama Canal, one of the most strategic stations, which regulates the flow of water traffic between the Atlantic and Pacific oceans. Great Britain has controlled the gates of Gibraltar as well as traffic through the Suez Canal. They have controlled the trading routes through the Khyber pass and areas in the Atlantic, Pacific and the Indian ocean.

Both Great Britain and the United States have ships and sea craft today patrolling the waters of the major oceans and seas of the world. We have and still are a predominant force for enforcing the customs and laws of the neutral waters and land of the world.

All the earth to be blessed with the Advent of Jesus Christ

The third part of the above prophecy stating; "In thy seed shall all nations of the earth be blessed" refers to the advent of Jesus Christ who came into the world to offer salvation to all; saints and sinner alike. Jesus Christ, counted as the seed of Abraham, freely offers the greatest blessing ever offered to mankind; that they may have eternal life through his sacrifice on the cross. News of this gift has spread around the world through missionary efforts and the King James Bible and is still offered freely to one and all!

Rebekah Promised Many Millions of Descendents

Rebekah, who was to become the wife of Isaac, was given a patriarchal blessing before departing her family; that her descendants would be huge in numbers that would be countless (Genesis 24:60):

"And they blessed Rebekah, and said unto her, thou *art* our sister, be thou *the mother* of thousands of millions, and let thy seed possess the gate of those which hate them."

And, of course, this blessing has been manifested down through the ages including today as it was passed on to Isaac and Jacob and to the descendants of Israel.

Naturally we can't claim there are thousands of millions of descendants of Israel living on earth at this time, but there are hundreds of millions living in various countries today. Descendants of Israel have been and are still residing in familiar countries today; to include the United States of America, Great Britain, the Scandinavian countries, Australia, New Zealand, Canada, Iceland, Germany, Asia, and other countries. You just can't fit all of these tribes of Israel into today's Middle Eastern country called Israel. As we have pointed out before, some of

61

today's clergy have said the gathering of Israel has been completed. Of course they are wrong. The massive exodus has not even gotten started good yet.

Great promises have been given to the descendants of Jacob (Israel) as recorded in Genesis 48: 1-16:

"And it came to pass after these things, that one told Joseph, Behold thy father is sick: and he took with him his two sons, Manasseh and Ephraim.

"And one told Jacob, and said, Behold thy son Joseph cometh unto thee; and Israel strengthened himself, and sat upon the bed.

"And Jacob said unto Joseph, God Almighty appeared before me at Luz in the land of Canaan and blessed me,

"And said unto me, Behold I will make thee fruitful and multiply thee, and I will make of thee a multitude of people; I will give this land to thy seed after thee *for* an everlasting possession.

"And now thy two sons, Ephraim and Manasseh, which were born unto thee in the land of Egypt before I came to thee in the land of Egypt, are mine; as Reuben and Simeon they shall be mine."

Jacob, in the preceding verses, is claiming the two sons of Joseph as full tribes of the Twelve Tribes of Israel with equal separate tribal status as Reuben, Simeon and all of the other tribes of Israel. The tribal count is now thirteen tribes of Israel.

We continue with Jacob's blessings on Ephraim and Manasseh:

"And Jacob beheld Joseph's sons and said, Who are these.

"And Joseph said unto his father, They are my sons, who God hath given me in this *place*. And he said, Bring them I pray thee unto me, and I will bless them.

"Now the eyes of Israel were dim for age, so that he could not see. And he brought them near unto him, and he kissed them and embraced them.

"And Joseph brought them out from between his knees, and he bowed himself with his face to the earth.

"And Joseph took them both, Ephraim in his right hand toward Israel's left hand and Manasseh in his left hand toward Israel's right hand, and brought them near unto him.

And Israel stretched out his right hand and laid it upon Ephraim's head, who was the younger, and his left hand upon Manasseh's head, guiding his hands wittingly; for Manasseh was the firstborn.

"And he blessed Joseph, and said, God before whom my fathers Abraham and Isaac did walk, the God which fed me all my life long unto this day.

"And the angel which redeemed me from evil, bless the Lads; and let my name be named on them, and the name of my fathers Abraham and Isaac, and let them grow into a multitude in the midst of the earth."

Ephraim and Manasseh were at this time given the title, Israel, as well as the names of Abraham and Isaac. No other tribes were given the title, *Israel.* The title was not given to the Jews as today's clergy teach.

Note in verse14 that Israel guided his hands wittingly. Israel had to cross his arms to place his hands as they were to give the right hand blessing (the most dominant) to Ephraim. To some, the crossed arms became the symbol of the tribe of Ephraim.

We continue with verse 17 through verse 20:

"And when Joseph saw that his father laid his right hand upon the head of Ephraim, it displeased him: and he held his father's hand to remove it from Ephraim's head to Manasseh's head.

"And Joseph said unto his father, Not so, father; for this is the firstborn; put thy right hand upon his head.

"And his father refused, and said, I know it my son, I know it; he also shall become a people, and he shall be great; but truly his younger brother shall be greater than he, and his seed shall become a multitude of nations.

"And he blessed them that day, saying, In thee shall Israel bless, saying God make thee as Ephraim and Manasseh; and he set Ephraim before Manasseh."

We must note here that the prophetic blessing on Ephraim and Manasseh was that Ephraim would become a multitude of nations or in our words today; *a commonwealth of nations.* Manasseh was to become a great nation.

There was never a nation of nations in Israel or elsewhere until Great Britain formed the British Commonwealth of Nations and spread around the world. America became the greatest nation on earth, fulfilling the prophecy as stated above.

Like Father, Like Son

As we have learned, the house of Israel was very massive in number and through Jacob, the tribes of Israel grew into multitudes in the earth. We also have learned through the Book of Genesis that Jacob fathered 12 sons and one daughter named Diana. Tribes were named after the heads of each of the sons; or the 12 sons of Israel. We are familiar with the plight of Joseph, one of the youngest of the sons of Jacob who was sold into slavery to the Egyptians by his brothers. Joseph antagonized his brothers by telling them about his dream that they would bow down to him. Joseph was the favorite son of all the sons of Israel. He was highly favored by Jacob. Jacob loved Joseph so much he made him a coat of many colors. Some read this as a prophetic sign that his descendents would be from many cultures and races, and being the seed of Israel would cause them the reap some of the blessings promised to the Ephraim and Manasseh.

As Joseph lived in Egypt he was favored by the Lord and was able to interpret dreams of the Pharaoh of Egypt. His interpretation of Pharaoh's dreams resulted in Egypt and other nations escaping famine. He was favored by the Pharaoh and given the rulership second only to the Pharaoh and was very prominent in the development of Egypt.

Joseph's brothers as well as Jacob were allowed to live in Egypt at the time and they prospered there. Without knowing who Joseph was, his brothers did bow down to him which fulfilled the prophecy of Genesis 37:8. Joseph set up a seven year storage of grains for the population and had enough food and provender for all Egypt and surrounding nations. Joseph saved many from starvation.

As we have shown, the dual blessings on Ephraim and Manasseh have blossomed into today's countries of Great Britain and America. America and Great Britain have reaped the majority blessings of the earth. We have owned a massive portion of the wealth of the world. Thus, we are not gentiles as most would suppose and believe. We are direct descendents, for the most part, of the House of Israel.

And, like father, like son, The United States and Great Britain have learned the lessons of Joseph while he was in Egypt, and have great stores of necessities for life, including food for their own survival as well as excess to feed other nations. The eastern nations of Europe and Russia are indebted to us for our generosity to prevent starvation of their own populations. This is characteristic of great nations that have the hand of God, their Creator, in their midst. We have made our enemies, once conquered, rich on goods as well as aid and technology. We have attacked Afghanistan's evil Taliban leaders and destroyed the evil government and at the same time dropping food to thousands upon thousands of their citizens by flyovers to keep them from starving. We have compassion for others and place high values on human lives. Heathen nations do not understand this, but it's exactly what God would have us do. As Christ taught; Love your Enemies!

Most citizens of this nation, The United States of America, are white English speaking and are descendents of Manasseh. Others of color also are of the seed of Manasseh, Israel, Isaac, and Abraham, and finally all the way back to Adam, Then we remember Joseph's coat of many colors, likely a prophetic sign to the different races to be found in the Tribes of Israel.

Promises for Latter Days

Jacob's prophetic promises made to the descendants of Israel specify the latter days as the fulfillment time of some of the prophecies. In Genesis 49:1-2 Jacob outlines his prophecy for our present time:

"And Jacob called unto his sons, and said, Gather yourselves together, that I may tell that which shall befall you in the LAST DAYS.

"Gather yourselves together, and hear, ye sons of Jacob; and hearken unto Israel your father"

Pay close attention to the time Jacob is addressing; THE LAST DAYS. This also can be called the latter days. We are talking about TODAY. What Jacob is going to describe is taking place presently in our own time and age.

This is a specific prophecy made to Joseph which was and is to be manifested in the tribes of Ephraim and Manasseh unto which the title *Israel* was given (Genesis 48:14-16). We continue with Genesis 49:22-26:

"Joseph is a fruitful bough, even a fruitful bough by a well; whose branches run over the wall.

"The archers have sorely grieved him, and shot at him, and hated him.

"but his bow abode in strength, and the arms of his hands were made strong by the hands of the mighty God of Jacob; (from thence is the shepherd, the stone of Israel;)

"Even by the God of thy fathers, who shall help thee; and by the Almighty who bless thee with blessings of heaven above, blessings of the deep that lieth under, blessings of the breast and blessings of the womb.

"The blessings of thy fathers have prevailed above the blessings of my progenitors unto the utmost bound of the everlasting hills; they shall be on the head of Joseph and on the crown of the head of him that was separate from his brethren."

These material blessings is upon the head of Ephraim and Manasseh, the two sons of Joseph, who hold the birthright. The prophecy is identifying the nations of the earth who are and will receive these blessings. As we did in the first chapter of this book, we are using the identifying signs and characteristics of the nation unto which the above prophecy applies.

Great Nations Identified

We have identified a nation that has been blessed with the ability to produce all things for use by all nations around the world; a country that has fed the world with their vast breadbasket. The land that has provided the ingenuity and technology to make life easier in all aspects; food, industry, transportation and providing all material needs of life. This is a country rich in all natural resources.

That nation is America; a nation whose enemies have waged war with them both at home and around the world and are still causing them grief. The nation has a mighty military force which has succeeded in all attacks and won all wars fought. The nation's military might was provided by the arm of God.

The nation has had the blessing of the heavens, the earth and the fruit of the breasts and of the womb. Rains have been provided in due season for the growth of agricultural products. The elements of the earth were available to include fuels, minerals for use in industry, agriculture and other areas. America is blessed with many descendants and massive populations. We continue to be blessed beyond what our ancestry have enjoyed. Our nation's blessings have increased in the many material things and technology is growing on a daily basis.

Yes, that nation is America! There is no other that compares; and certainly not today's middle eastern nation called Israel!

Considering the great country in which we live – the United States of America – one must be overly impressed and even awed at the magnificence of this great land! It's as if a great providential being determined greatness upon this continent. And He did! We have the very best of everything. We have an overabundance of food and minerals and have no needs that this country cannot provide materially. Our country is located in a temperate zone that provides weather needed for agricultural overabundance of everything we have undertaken. We have absolutely the very best of everything materially. We are located between two oceans and the north and the south poles and out of the way of prolonged attacks on American soil from any of our enemies.

If we could look from far above the earth, we could see the continent of America and that the United States has been divided into zones for the different products we enjoy and also provide to other countries around the world.

We have grain from the wheat fields of the mid-west which supplies food for many nations. Corn is in such abundance, we have started making fuel for our cars and trucks as well as tractors and farm machinery with the excess. Cattle and sheep from the western states is overabundant. Milk is so plentiful we have poured it away just to get rid of it. We have dumped potatoes into the ocean because of the overabundance.

In the north of this great nation we have dairy products that are used all around the world. The United States produces more cheese than any country on earth. Sugar cane and beets are abundant in the western states and Hawaii. We have rice from South Carolina, Louisiana and Arkansas, also in abundance. Our rice crops rival that of China!.

We have the fruited plains of California, Oregon and Washington as well as fruits grown in the New England states where we have apples, pears, grapes, etc. These are also very much in abundance.

The volcanic soils of Washington, Idaho and Colorado produce bumper crop after bumper crop of potatoes. One becomes overwhelmed when considering the many potatoes and potato products that are consumed daily - almost a staple of the American family diet. Potatoes are a native product and have been adopted by all cultures and nations of the world.

Tropical states such as California, Florida and Hawaii produce most of our citrus fruits as well as other fruits and early crops to be used before our temperate areas get into full production.

As part of our Free Trade Agreements, South America, Mexico and other foreign countries produce some of the fruits and vegetables we use. We do not need them! Of course this is a world wide political scheme of which we provide the most support. We don't need these products as we have the very best of everything grown. We import beef, pork and other meats from foreign countries, yet we export some of the same. Our trade agreements are one sided in favor of others. This is a political scheme of which we Americans should have no part of. It's being pushed upon us by some of the more envious nations of the world.

This nation has always been free with our over-abundance of all things allowing other nations to partake but we get no reciprocation nor consideration from others. It's as if we owe them and they expect it!

We have coal and other mined minerals from Kentucky, West Virginia, Pennsylvania and western states. We have precious metals from Nevada, California and Alaska. Metals such as these are used in communications in the space exploration as well as delicate connections in submarines and civilian industry not to mention jewelry and the currency we use.

We have great forests of timber from the northwestern areas.

We have minerals and salt from the western deserts. We have oil and natural gas reserves in virtually every state within this great nation.

We have our industrial areas in almost all parts of this nation. We pioneered nuclear power systems as well as nuclear propulsion for aircraft carriers and submarines.

Banking and commerce flourish in all large cities.

We have a central democratic government that is copied by many countries of the world. Our stock market has been the forerunner of all investment interests.

We have been blessed with many treasures from the heavens that give us our growing seasons as well as the comfort seasons of the year. We have saved many nations from starvation and provided funds for their national relief from weather related or other catastrophes. We are the country all nations look to for help when they have a need and we freely give. We have fed the very enemies of this nation knowing well they would destroy us if given the opportunity.

We are the last surviving superpower of this age which is coming to a close. Our military might is the greatest that ever has been. Our technologies are sought around the world. Our learning institutions are sought by foreign citizens from every country. Our medical technology and facilities, research, and hospitals are a model for all to see. And our space age technologies have sent men to the moon and back several times over.

We monitor the world for earthquake activity with our seismographic apparatus. We provide weather information with our weather monitoring systems. We are among the first to get involved when there is an international catastrophe such as earthquakes and tsunamis, volcanic eruptions, flooding and other natural disasters.

We have experienced the industrial revolution involving America and Great Britain within the last 200 plus years or more that has been unrivaled by anything existing anywhere. This is when the technical age began. We have been the leader in all technology.

Together, America and Great Britain have given the world almost every conceivable invention, contrivance, method, apparatus and technology to advance all nations to progress in our needed time. We take credit for many, many things, yet we know God has given freely of all things to the nations of Israel. God is the author of all good things of this earth. It is He that has caused our very abundant blessings and progress in all things.

We know that we are the envy of every nation on earth. All nations seek what we have and some achieve but never to the greatness of the United States of America! Some nations would seek to destroy us for out great blessings poured out by our Creator.

We have freedoms in our country which others can only dream about. The prices we pay for all products, including gasoline, is the least expensive of any country.

The United States along with Great Britain have provided stability for the whole world. Together we have controlled the waterways and passages of all of the world. We control the Canals and straits of the oceans. We have fought wars and later given financial aid and construction for rebuilding the nations and setting up democratic governments causing former enemy nations to become wealthy. We have aided our former enemies, Japan and Germany, to flourish and advance to become among the richer nations on earth.

Lest we gloat, the Lord has given all of this to us as he has promised in Gen. 49. We have welcomed those from oppression through our immigration services. We have been a watchdog for other countries leading citizens of countries to fight for freedoms.

Great Britain has translated the Authorized King James bible and through missionary work Great Britain and America have had Christian missionaries around the world spreading the good news to all who will receive.

The might of the United States and Great Britain is overwhelming and awesome to say the least. We have surpassed all of the blessings pronounced on Ephraim and Manasseh, both sons of Joseph per the characteristics found in the prophecy of Genesis 49:22-26.

We simply ask: Is there a nation on earth today that meets the characteristics of the above referenced scriptures? Many, including some of our most renowned evangelists think the regathering in Israel has been completed. This is most emphatically not true and shows a pronounced clerical ignorance of biblical history.

If we believe we are living in the end times we must find the nations of today that meet the prophecies of Gen. 49 which was promised Ephraim and Manasseh. Many assume these nations are located in today's Israel in the middle east. This is not the case. It is America and Great Britain; not the little Israel in the middle east. The Jewish state does not meet the characteristics of this end time prophecy by any means. There is no doubt we are today's true Israel.

America and Great Britain are the latter day Israel spoken of by Jacob (Israel) in Gen. 49:22-26. Great Britain was the fore-runner until they became more or less weakened by many wars in their long existence. The last two world wars have taken a toll on Great Britain's youth and world dominance and has taken away her ability to become a major end time world power. For a great while the whole world was under British dominance as was promised in Gen. 48, that they would be-come a nation of nations - the British Commonwealth of Na-tions. We are still allied as brothers for the protection of our freedoms and will always fight side by side in any effort to the free countries of the world from outside threats to their free-doms.

Other allies have fallen away and no longer fight for the free-dom of the world for which we have fought and sacrificed. We have freed all of Europe from the threat of becoming a Nazi empire, and have made Germany a premier nation.

We have freed France from domination during the past 2 world wars. The graves of fallen Americans attest to our sacrifices to France. Now there is no support from France and Germany for our quest to keep the nations safe from terrorists round the world. There is very little concern from the so called allies for the losses we have suffered through the terrorists activities. We are engaged in a war in Iraq which is being aided by very few nations of the world. Our action in Iraq is designed to stop terrorism in that nation rather than letting it spread to our na-tion where our families can be killed and cities destroyed.

Other nations run to us for aid in their troubled times. We can not get our closest neighbor, Canada, to stand by us. Rather they ridicule our actions while we sacrifice our own young men and provide military protection from our own nation should they be attacked. Canada, the American representative of Ephraim, has taken the lead of Charles DeGaulle and is now one of our most outstanding critics. Still, the world knows the heart of America. They know we stand ready to provide help to all nations of the world should a need arise.

This nation is the unique nation Jacob speaks of in Gen. 49. We are that nation that will afford the protection to other nations and share in the resources of this great land.

CHAPTER Six
Israel in the Millenium

Israel will be called upon to play an important role in the millennium. They will be sealed and commissioned to teach and bring to pass the truths that God has presented before us in the last 2000 years.. Christ had a short ministry which lasted approximately three and a half years and taught the new covenant that God had promised in Ezekiel 37:26:

"Moreover I will make a covenant of peace with them; it shall be an everlasting covenant with them: and I will place them, and multiply them, and will set my Sanctuary in the midst of them for evermore."

This is the great covenant of peace the Lord has promised for those who would obey his commandments.

Revelation 7:9-14 describes a multitude no man could number

who stood before the throne of God and before the Lamb clothed in white robes:

"After this I beheld, and, lo, a great multitude, which no man could number, of all nations, and kindreds and people and tongues, stood before the throne, and before the Lamb, clothed with white robes, and palms in their hands;

"And cried with a loud voice, saying, Salvation to our God which sitteth upon the throne, and to the Lamb.

"And all the angels stood round about the throne, and about the elders and the four beasts, and fell before the throne on their faces , and worshipped God.

"Saying, Amen: Blessing, and glory, and wisdom, and thanksgiving, and honor and power, and might, *be* unto our God for ever and ever, Amen.

"And one of the elders answered, saying unto me, What are these which are arrayed in white robes? and whence came they?

"And I said unto him, Sir, thou knowest. And he said unto me, these are they which came out of the great tribulation and have washed their robes, and made them white in the blood of the Lamb."

Again this multitude that no man could number went through the tribulation and were persecuted and many shed their blood unto death for the word of God.

Israel to be Sealed

The fact that one hundred and forty four thousand saints selected from the tribes of Israel to be sealed - twelve thousand from each tribe - to be God's servants and ministers on earth proves beyond doubt the Tribes of Israel still reside here on earth in various countries during the great tribulation.

Twelve thousand members of each tribe totaling 144 thousand will be called out and sealed in their forehead (Revelation 7:2-4):

"And I saw another angel ascending from the east, having the seal of the living God: and he cried with a loud voice to the four angels, to whom it was given to hurt the earth and the sea,

"Saying, Hurt not the earth neither the sea, nor the trees, till we have sealed the servants of our God in their foreheads.

"And I heard the number of them which were sealed an hundred and forty and four thousand of all the tribes of the children of Israel."

The sealing of the one hundred and forty four thousand gives them power and credentials and will guarantee their safety while they are doing the millennial works of God on earth. They cannot be harmed while performing the work of the Lord. They will spread the true gospel of God as opposed to traditions and man made doctrine. Many will decide their salvation during this period.

Those selected and sealed will be taken from the 12 tribes of Israel; twelve thousand from each tribe as shown:

Judah, twelve thousand
Gad, twelve thousand
Naphthalim, twelve thousand

Simeon, twelve thousand
Issachar, twelve thousand

Reuben, twelve thousand
Asher, twelve thousand
Manasseh, twelve thousand

Levi, twelve thousand
Zebulon, twelve thousand

Benjamin, twelve thousand   Joseph, twelve thousand

Some clergy and scholars falsely claim all of the sealed ones are Jews. Obviously, this can not be true according to the above stated scripture. This is another instance where the clergy is confusing Jews with the House of Israel. Let us state again; Jews do not in any way constitute the whole House of Israel! The Jews are merely one tribe, and only one tribe, of the House of Israel. They are not the largest tribes. The term Jew is a nickname for the tribe of Judah. They are known to-day because they kept the true Sabbath, but, they do not own the title Israel. As we have repeated, the title, Israel, was given to Ephraim and Manasseh, the two sons of Joseph (Gen.48:16).

Since these tribes to be sealed were appointed by Jesus Christ, they must be Christian in belief and can not be teaching Jewish doctrine. Those sealed ones will be teaching Christian doctrine but likely not today's doctrines but rather the real truth. The tribe of Judah (Jews) is included in those to be sealed. They will be teaching Christian principles All of the tribes of Israel will be teaching true Christian doctrine.

All Israel will be Saved

Conspicuously absent from the tribes to be sealed is the tribe of Dan and the tribe of Ephraim. Joseph is often substituted for the tribe of Ephraim. Levi who had no inheritance is being substituted for the tribe of Dan. Some bible students and clergy believe Dan was omitted because he was the first to set up idols to worship in Samaria after the separation of Judah from the Ten Tribes of Israel. The omission of some tribes will not affect the promises and gifts given after the tribulation and in the millennium. As the bible states in Romans 11: 26-29:

"And so all Israel shall be saved; as it is written, there shall come out of Sion the Deliverer, and shall turn away ungodliness from Jacob (Israel).

"For this is my covenant unto them, when I shall take away their sins.

"As concerning the gospel, they are enemies for your sakes; but as for touching the election, they are beloved for the Father's sakes,

"For the gifts and calling of God are without repentance."

Those with the seal of God in their forehead will be scattered around the world to where the tribes of Israel reside. Twelve thousand for all counties with tribal inhabitation - France, Great Britain, the Netherlands, Germany, America and others.

The sealed ones will not be teaching doctrine of today's popular denominations. There are hundreds of denominations and they differ in their beliefs. This will be an entirely new game. The protestants of today, as well as other Christian denominations have denied some of the truths of the Bible and are teaching some of the old traditions, customs and man made doctrines which have been around for years that have no place in the bible.

Obviously, the millennium will be a great time of correction. Traditions which have no root in the word of God will be cast aside; as will myriads of odd practices adopted by man to benefit a select group Everybody on earth will have an opportunity to accept or deny the truth.

Christian churches are on the decline. We are under regulations from our government that are taking away our Christian practices and beliefs. The founders of this great nation surely did not form a nation as paganized as we are today. Since

1960, we have fallen away from the standards of our higher moral society.

Our Forefathers Extolled Higher Values

The Supreme Court of this land originally adopted the Ten Commandments to regulate law in this land. Near the top of the Supreme Court building one can see a row of lawgivers featuring Moses, the lawgiver of the Old Testament, displaying the Ten Commandments.

The Ten commandments are prominent in the Supreme Court Building, both inside and out. The laws of our government originally was based on the Ten Commandments. Other buildings in our government display the moral values as well as the Commandments. Our motto; "In God We Trust" is still visible on government documents and coinage.

John Jay, our first Supreme Court Justice made the statement:

"Americans should select and prefer Christians as their rulers."

Patrick Henry emphasized this government was founded on Christian principles:

"It can not be emphasized too strongly or too often that this great nation was founded not by religionists but by Christians, not on religions, but on the Gospel of Jesus Christ."

Even Winston Churchill, Prime Minster of England during World War II noticed some of the greatness of our country:

"He must indeed have a blind soul who cannot see that some great purpose and design is being worked out here below of which we have the honor to be the faithful servants."

Of course, Winston Churchill is a descendant of Ephraim who holds the title, *Israel*, along with Manasseh, whose descendents are America. Most of our earlier patriots had expressed similar thoughts about our democratic way of life.

James Monroe advocated a government according to biblical principles:

"We have staked the whole of our political institutions upon the capacity of mankind for self government, upon the capacity of each and all of us to govern ourselves, to control ourselves to sustain ourselves according to the Ten Commandments of God."

As we can very plainly see, our country had a Christian beginning. Most patriots of this nation have voiced their belief in a Christian way of life.

But, alas, the Supreme Court as well as the courts of this land and the Civil Liberties Union has taken away our right to worship as we please with their rulings in favor of abortion, homosexuality, pornography, gay marriage, and abandonment of the Ten Commandments and public prayer. The Supreme Court should be tending to their business of interpreting the laws rather than making them. The high standards previously practiced by our society have dipped to the very bottom within the last 50 years as was predicted and prophesied in the Holy Bible. Abandonment of the principles given by the Lord carries heavy penalties as we have Seen in Deuteronomy 28 and Leviticus 26 of the Holy Bible.

The Sabbath Day

Most Christian churches have fallen away from the Ten Commandments which they say they observe. They recognize only nine commandments; disregarding the fourth commandment which deals with the Sabbath day as follows:

"Remember the Sabbath day to keep it holy."

Obviously, they worship on the Catholic Sabbath. Observance of the Sabbath on Sunday is in no way authorized by God. As a matter of record, Jesus, Himself, said he would not change even a jot or tittle until all things were fulfilled as shown in Matt. 5:17-19:

"Think not that I am come to destroy the law, or the prophets; I am not come to destroy, but to fulfill.

"For verily I say unto you till heaven and earth pass, one jot or one tittle shall in no wise pass from the law, till all be fulfilled.

"Whosoever therefore shall break one of these least commandments, and shall teach men so, he shall be called the least in the kingdom of heaven; but whosoever shall do and teach *them*, the same shall be called great in the kingdom of heaven."

This seems to be a pretty severe warning to the pastors and teachers of our churches today as they pay no attention whatever to this warning. It glides right over their heads. It's basically saying that if you fail to teach the commandments as received by Moses from the Lord, you will be least in the kingdom of heaven. You may avoid this shame by preaching every word and tenet of the Ten Commandments and you will be called great.

The true Sabbath was originally set for the seventh day which is Saturday. We refer to Sunday worship the Catholic Sabbath because they are the ones who changed from the true Sabbath to Sunday. This change was made at the council of Laodicea in 364 AD because of pressure from a pseudo Christian named Constantine I. Constantine made the change in 321 AD to fit his pagan god worship. This change was in no way authorized by the Lord who established it. The protestant world has recognized Sunday worship from that time. There are some that still revere the true Sabbath as was originally set by God. The true Sabbath will be restored during the millennium when the kingdom of God is established on earth. As the Lord said, He would not change one jot or one tittle!

CHAPTER Seven
More Phrophecies by Jeremiah

Bible scholars have divided the Bible into parts with prophecy accounting for one third of written scripture. Thus, we have more prophecy to unveil to complete what is in store for those of us living on earth today.

We have covered the most prominent prophecies of Ezekiel which identifies the nations of Israel and Russia in our own day and age as well as today's Judah. We have touched upon other prophecies made by Ezekiel regarding our future. We also have covered some of the prophecies by Jeremiah which explained how the Kingdom of Israel was overturned three times installing the ruling descendents of Judah to the Isles of Great Britain.

Jeremiah's End Time Prophecy

Prophecies by Jeremiah covering events and catastrophes that will take place in the end time regarding Israel, Jerusalem and the nation of Babylon loom ahead. Today's Babylon is situated in Iraq close to the city of Baghdad. The Biblical Chaldeans are today's citizens of Iraq and perhaps some of Iran. The Biblical Babylon is today's Iraq including Baghdad.

On September 11, 2001, the United States was attacked by Muslim terrorists with our own 767 sized passenger planes. Two of the planes were flown into the twin towers of the World Trade Canter in New York stunning the whole world and killing more than 3000 people from nations around the world.   Another plane failed and went down in a field in Pennsylvania. Reportedly, this plane was headed to Washington for a strike on the center of government - and more likely the white house. Pres. George W. Bush was in a grade school in Florida when he heard of the attacks. The fourth airliner crashed into the Pentagon destroying part of one of the sides of the pentagon shaped office building of the Department of Defense. Several people on the ground were killed as well as all on the attacking plane.

We have since re-established our security for airline travel costing many millions of dollars to install, set up and train security personnel. The airline industry has lost millions in revenues. Our government has developed a Homeland Security office and hired thousands in this and related protective security branches of the government.

Following the attack and the destruction of the twin towers in New York and the crash into the Pentagon, the President of the United States declared a state of war on worldwide terrorism which included Muslims from the Arab states. The 9/11 attacks were engineered by Osama Bin Laden from inside Afghanistan. Shortly after, the United States went to war with Afghanistan in an effort to find and bring to justice Bin Laden who funded and led the attack against the United States. The Taliban government of Afghanistan was destroyed by the military forces of America and their brother nation of Great Britain along with a hand full of allies.

America Goes to War

A short time later we sought a declaration of war from the United Nations to invade Iraq which we believed held weapons of mass destruction. We did not get the full support of the United Nations and recruited our allies which included America, Great Britain, Spain, Italy, Japan, and other nations. The nations of France and Germany and a few other nations chose not to participate because of invested interests in Iraq.

The overthrow of Iraq took place in record time with highly intelligent leaders, strategists and precision weaponry.

We are now in control of Iraq and in the process of helping them set up a Democracy. The original goal was to oust Saddam Hussein from Iraq and install a democratic government in the very middle of the Arab nations where we would not be under constant threat of terrorist states and to afford an American Military base of operations.

Oil likely was an influencing factor in the quest to set up a democracy in Iraq.

The overthrow of Iraq was justified as well as the raid on Afghanistan. The US through these two operations have wiped out a lot of terrorists and kept America from being continuously raided. We have sharpened our defenses against terrorism. Many have been overly critical regarding the war, but it has produced results. It's almost time for the war in Iraq to cease and allow the Iraqi government to take over the military operations and bring Americans back home. It's evident from the prophecy of Jeremiah, DEMOCRACY WILL NOT PREVAIL IN IRAQ!

According to the prophet Jeremiah, the democracy in Iraq will not last. The nation will likely be under democratic rule from within for a time but will not last as we read in Jeremiah 50:1-3:

Publish and conceal not:

"The word that the Lord spoke against Babylon and against the land of Chaldeans And by Jeremiah the prophet.

"Declare ye among the nations, and publish and set up a standard; publish , and conceal not: say, Babylon is taken, Bel is confused, Merodach is broken in pieces; Her idols are broken in pieces.

"For out of the north there cometh up a nation against her, which shall make her land desolate, and none shall dwell therein: they shall remove, they shall depart, both man and beast."

The Lord is commanding Jeremiah to let the world know what is coming to the Babylonian kingdom which is identified today as Iraq and Baghdad and her citizens. They will virtually be wiped out with weapons by modern day Israel and Judah.

A great nation out of the north will attack and destroy Babylon and the Chaldeans. The destruction will be as final as the words of Jeremiah 1:3: "…which shall make her land desolate, and none shall dwell therein…"

The Final Event for Iraq

This will be a final destruction of the land and none will ever be able to live there again. This indicates the final destruction, which has not yet happened, is looming over Iraq and will happen as the prophecy indicates. Prophecy of the Bible has happened as it's time has approached. It will happen as prophesied.

The coalition forces, consisting of America, Great Britain and their allies, are in control of Iraq today and working diligently to set up a democracy that will not be accepted in a Muslim or Arab country. This land has always been ruled under a dictator or king. Democracies are not popular in the middle east.

The weapons of war to wipe out Iraq and the Chaldeans will be weapons of mass destruction as we have heard re-echoed around the world for several years and as shown in Jeremiah 50:39:

"Therefore the wild beasts of the desert with the wild beast of the islands shall dwell *there,* and the owls shall dwell therein; and it shall be no more inhabited forever; neither shall it be dwelt in from generation to generation."

This attests to the finality of the destruction. We are talking about many nuclear devices and all manner of germ and chemical warfare.

And who will be the invader who will destroy this land and why?

The Lord is warning in Jeremiah 50:8-9 of the swift destruction by forces from the north:

"Move from the midst of Babylon. Go out of the land of the Chaldeans; And be like the rams before the flocks.

"For behold, I will raise and cause to come up against Babylon an assembly of great nations from the north country…"

Thus Babylon (or in today's language, Iraq and Baghdad) will be attacked from the north.

The Lord has named Judah and Israel as shown in Jeremiah 51:19-21 as the destroyers who will destroy the nation of Iraq:

"The portion of Jacob is not like them, for He is the Maker of all things; And Israel is the tribe of His inheritance. The Lord of hosts is His name.

"You are my battle axe *and* weapons of war: For with you I will break the nation Into pieces. With you I will destroy kingdoms;"

Thus it becomes absolute; the nation of Iraq will not prevail as the Lord has designs against it. Iraq will become a desolation without habitation as Sodom and Gomorrah is today.

The nation of Iraq is presently setting up a democratic government consisting of several Islamic groups which oppose each other. The Shiites seem to be the biggest group with the Sunni second. The Kurds in the north are also a very powerful force and their expertise seem to be military.

A government of several coalition groups likely will be infighting from now until they are destroyed from the face of the earth. It would do America well to begin withdrawing our forces from Iraq. If not, we will be tied to them until they are overrun and destroyed. The war is estimated to cost from one trillion to two trillion for us to insure peace and democracy there. Why are we setting up a democracy when ancient prophets predict the complete destruction there?

Iran, today's Persia, also will get in on the end of time action. They are developing atomic weaponry and are a threat to the whole world and likely will be wiped out by Israel if by nobody else.

CHAPTER Eight
The Giants of Genesis Six

Are there giants mentioned in the Bible? We remember David slew a giant named Goliath with a pebble from a sling. As written in Genesis 6:1-8:

"And it came to pass, when men began to multiply on the face of the earth, and daughters were born unto them,

"That the sons of God saw the daughters of men that they were fair; and they took them wives of all which they chose.

"And the Lord said, My spirit will not always strive with man, for he also is flesh: yet his days shall be an hundred and twenty years.

"There were giants in the earth in those days; and also after that, when the sons of God came in unto the daughters of men, and they bare *children* to them, the same became mighty men which were old, men of renown.

"And God saw that the wickedness of man *was* great in the earth, and *that* every imagination of the thoughts of his heart *was* only evil continually.

"And it repented the Lord that he had made man on earth, and it grieved him at his heart.

"And the Lord said I will destroy man whom I have created from the face of the earth; both man and beast, and the creeping thing, and the fowls of the air; for it repenteth me that I have made them."

The giants were the descendents of the fallen angels and called Nephilim and were apparently great in size and great in evil. They created all manner of evil acts upon the inhabitants including the beasts and fed themselves unto the destruction of earthlings. They created barbaric acts, fornication, cannibalism, destruction and introduced ungodly practices. Some grew to monumental size and were to be destroyed from the face of the earth by a flood.

Apparently there was a second influx according to the above scripture: "there were giants in the earth in those days; AND ALSO AFTER THAT," as experienced by the children of Israel when they went to spy out Canaan, the land that was to become their inheritance.

The Lord commanded Moses to send out spies into the land of Canaan which was to become the inheritance for the children of Israel. Moses sent them out by tribes, each tribe a representative, to spy out the land. So, they went out from the wilderness of Zin as far as Rehob and and to Hebron. When reaching the valley of Eshcol they cut down a branch with only one cluster of grapes which took two men to carry. They returned after forty days of exploring the land. and reported to Moses. The tribal representatives did not want to possess the land because they were frightened by the size of the inhabitants.

The inhabitants were giants who devoured their own and were of Anak. They reported the size of the giants were several times larger than the spies comparing their own size as grasshoppers. Joshua and Caleb reported the land was fertile and they believed the children of Israel could take it, but the children balked. And as a result, only Caleb and Joshua were permitted to go over into the promised land. Others who did not want to take the land wandered in the desert until they all died. When the time came for the possession, the giants were to be destroyed by the Israelites.

For this reason, God commanded the armies of Israel to go into the land and destroy every inhabitant of the land including the men, women and children and even their livestock in some instances; as the giants also committed evil acts with animals and were cannibalistic. The evil inhabitants were to be cut off, driven out and utterly destroyed from all countries Israel was to inhabit. Some think God was an evil God to slay all inhabitants and even the children, but these were evil giants and their progeny, who would turn the whole earth to ungodly sin and all manner of violent acts. The giants were to have no resurrection and the fallen angels would receive no salvation but condemned to die for leaving heaven and coming to earth.

The Book of Enoch (not part of the King James Bible) is more detailed regarding the fallen angels:

From Sect 1, chapter V1-1 1-6:

"And it came to pass when the children of men had multiplied and in those days Were born unto them beautiful and comely daughters.

"And the angels, children of heaven, saw and lusted after them, and said one to another: come, let us choose us wives from among the children of man and beget us children.

"And Semjaza, who was their leader, said unto them: I fear ye will not indeed agree to do this deed, and I alone shall have to pay the penalty of a great sin.

"And they all answered him and said: Let us all swear an oath, and all bind ourselves by mutual imprecation not to abandon this plan but to do this thing.

"Then they sware they all together bound themselves by mutual imprecation upon it.

"And they were in all two hundred; who descended in the days of Jared on the summit of Mount Hermon, and they called it Mount Hermon, because they had sworn and bound themselves by mutual imprecation upon it."

From Sect 1, chapter V11-1 1-6

"And all the others together with them took unto themselves wives, and each chose for himself one, and they began to go in unto them and to defile themselves with them, and they taught them charms and enchantments, and the cutting of roots, and made them acquainted them with plants.

"And they became pregnant, and they bare great giants, whose height was three thousand ells;

"Who consumed all the acquisition of men. And when men could no longer sustain them.

"The giants turned against them and devoured mankind.

"And they began to sin against birds, and beasts, and reptiles, and fish, and to devour one another's flesh, and drink blood.

"Then the earth laid accusation against the lawless ones."

The version of Enoch used in the above was a translation from the Ethiopic Texts.

The five cities associated with Sodom and Gomorrah were filled with the giants who were called various names throughout the Bible. It was for this reason those cities were destroyed.

Fallen Angels to Return to Earth

According to Matthew 24:37-38, the earth will be visited by another influx of fallen angels to create the society of the giants:

"But as the days of No'-e (Noah) *were,* so shall also the coming of the Son of Man be."

"For in the days that were before the flood they were eating and drinking, Marrying and giving in marriage, the day that No'-e entered into the ark."

So, according to the above information we will be visited by the fallen angels and the earth will be again populated by the giants. Some of today's researchers have discovered graves of the giants and found skeletons belonging to those who were very tall and had to be giants when they roamed the earth. Some had six digits on their hands and feet. Some had double rows of teeth. We are talking about statures of more than twelve feet tall!

CHAPTER **Nine**

Biblical Phenomenon
Wise Men Guided by a Star

Most of us, during out growing up years, have experienced or taken part in a Christmas Pageant or play at our local church. The story goes that three wise man from the east journeyed to the place where Jesus was born in Bethlehem and were led by a star which shown down on the baby Jesus shortly after he was born. According to Matthew, these wise men traveled from the east, but there is no mention of "three" wise men. The scripture only says wise men which indicates more than one. It certainly could have been three - or - it could have been more! Since this event is not covered in the other three gospels (Mark, Luke and John), lets take a look at what Matthew is trying to get us to understand (Matt 2:1-6):

"Now when Jesus was born in Bethlehem of Judea in the days of Herod the king, behold there came wise men from the east to Jerusalem.

"Saying, where is he that is born King of the Jews? for we have seen his star in the east, and are come to worship him.

"When Herod the king had heard *these things*, he was troubled, and all Jerusalem with him,

"And when he had gathered all the chief priests and scribes of the people together, he demanded of them where Christ should be born.

"And they said unto him, In Beth'-le-hem of Ju-dae'-a ; for thus it is written by the prophet,

"And thou Bethlehem, *in* the land of Judah, art not thee least among the princes of Judah, for out of thee shall come a Governor, that shall rule my people Israel."

At the time king Herod was concerned that he would be supplanted by this new "King of the Jews" and sought to kill the babe.

The bible does not tell how long after the birth of Jesus before the wise men came to visit Him. It becomes questionable whether they visited Him the very night of His birth or at a later date in His home. If the wise men were in the east and were guided by a star, it's unlikely they were able to make it to Bethlehem that very night due to the lack of rapid transportation at that time. The wise men likely traveled by camels; and aren't they slow. They likely visited Jesus after the birth when He was in his home (Matthew 2:7-11)

"Then Herod, when he had privily called the wise men, enquired of them diligently what time the star appeared.

"And he sent them to Bethlehem, and said, Go and search diligently for the young child; when ye have found *him*, bring me word again, that I may come and worship him also.

"When they had heard the king, they departed; and lo, the star, which they saw in the east, went before them, till it came and stood over where the young child was.

When they saw the star, they rejoiced with exceeding great joy."

"And when they were come into the house, they saw the young child with Mary his mother, and fell down, and worshipped him: and when they opened their treasures, they presented unto him gifts; gold and frankincense and myrrh."

The wise men were warned of God that they should return to the east and not report to Herod, so they returned by a different route.

What was the star that was leading the wise men?

The star in our solar system is the sun! The scripture says "star" which is what the wise men thought it was. Obviously, it could not have been a star. A star such as our sun could not approach the earth without causing catastrophic consequences! Some Bible students say maybe it was a comet, or a meteorite, but huge bodies from the skies would all cause troublesome events to take place all around the earth. So, just what was the "Star" mentioned in this account? Surely, the wise men thought it was a star.

We must remember in this space age, we have studied the heavens as never before and have sent men to the moon. We have explored the universe for hundreds of years. In the subject time frame, most men didn't even know the earth was round and that planets revolved around the sun. The wise men, identified as astrologers and astronomers by some, had only vague ideas of the nature of space and the skies at this time.

Most Bible students and clergy are familiar with Ezekiel's description of a flying craft which we have discussed in Chapter 1 of this book and reported in Ezekiel 1:1. He has in his lifetime seen boats, barges and chariots but never anything such as this. Today, we call them UFO's or space ships. There are Many reported sightings of these crafts, such as Ezekiel witnessed, from all parts of the earth on a regular basis. Ezekiel gives details of transportation very few of us have seen, and this was long ago before anyone had ever heard of flying craft!

Flying Craft

We would suggest the "star" mentioned above was none other than a flying craft such as the one Ezekiel saw. A flying craft could easily have had a light shining down on the babe to illuminate the area for the wise men. If you believe the bible to be true, then you must believe Ezekiel saw a modern flying space craft with smaller attendant craft. He has described this event in detail in Ezekiel 1:1. God has many highly technical means of travel and technical things we will likely see in the future. He travels on occasion in a vehicle such as this. Ezekiel describes seeing the Lord in the mother ship above the earth as recorded in Ezekiel 1:26-28:

"And above the firmament that was over their heads *was* the likeness of a throne, as the appearance of a sapphire stone; and upon the likeness of the throne *was* the likeness as the appearance of a man above upon it.

"And I saw as the colour of amber, as the appearance of fire round about within it, from the appearance of his loins even upward, and from the appearance of his loins even downward, I saw as it were the appearance of fire, and it had brightness round about.

"As the appearance of the bow that is in the cloud in the day of rain, so *was* the appearance of the brightness round about. This *was* the appearance of the likeness of the glory of the Lord. And when I saw *it,* I fell upon my face, and I heard a voice of one that spake."

Enoch Taken by the Lord

Apparently, this mode of flying transportation has been around for some time. We have seen and read of other events which likely involved what we call flying space craft. We refer to Genesis 5:22-24:

"And E'noch walked with God after he begat Me-thu'-se-lah three hundred years and begat sons and daughters:

"And all the days of E'noch were three hundred and sixty five years.

"And E'noch walked with God: and he was not; for God took him."

The Bible does not say how he was taken and is very vague, but we can use our limited knowledge to surmise he was taken away inside of some mode of highly technical transportation much like Ezekiel has described.

Elijah Rides to Heaven in a Space Ship

The prophet Elijah in the days of the division of Israel also was taken by the Lord in a similar manner (II Kings 2:1):

"And it came to pass, when the Lord would take up Elijah into heaven by a whirlwind, that Elijah went with Elisha from Gilgal."

Elijah was traveling with Elisha who would succeed him as prophet in Israel. When Elijah asked Elisha to tarry while he went into some places, Elisha always answered by saying; "As the Lord liveth, and as thy soul liveth, I will not leave thee." As they journeyed to Jordan Elijah caused the waters to part (II Kings 2:8-11):

"And Elijah took his mantle and wrapped *it* together, and smote the waters, and they were divided hither and thither, so that they two went over on dry ground.

"And it came to pass, when they were gone over, that Elijah said unto Elisha, Ask what I shall do for thee, before I be taken away from thee. And Elisha said, I pray thee, let a double portion of thy spirit be upon me,

"And he said, thou hast asked a hard thing; *nevertheless,* if thou see me *when* I *am* taken from thee, it shall be so unto thee, but if not, it shall not be *so.*

"And it came to pass, as they still went on, and talked, that behold, *there appeared* a chariot of fire, and horses of fire, and parted them both asunder; and Elijah went up by a whirlwind into heaven."

Apparently the scripture is describing the flying craft as a *chariot of fire and horses of fire.* Never having witnessed any mode of transportation other than a horse and chariot, how else could they give a description of one being taken away into heaven? Again, at that time, no one had seen flying aircraft and their description is of a flying craft. Obviously, horses cannot fly and a chariot of fire is describing a craft that is being accelerated by the equivalent of modern day propulsion - or greater.

We who occasionally like to watch a western movie have seen the trains streak across the western prairie and go on to the west. The Indians called the train an *iron horse*. Of course this was in the style of Elijah's horse of fire. They surely weren't horses. Those who are not familiar with modern day transportation would not be able to describe something they had never before seen. We see this in our own day and age as those who have experienced a UFO first started calling them flying saucers.

Jacob's Ladder

Jacob had a vision of a ladder reaching to heaven with angels ascending and descending to and from the earth (Gen. 28:12 & 13):

"And he dreamed, and behold a ladder set up on the earth; and the top of it reached to heaven: And behold the angels of God ascending and descending on it.

"And, behold, the Lord stood above it, and said, I *am* the Lord God of Abraham thy father, and the God of Isaac: the land whereon thy liest to thee will I give it, and to thy seed."

Could Jacob have experienced a vision wherein he was looking at a space ship? Jacob was describing a ladder that reached all the way to heaven. Could heaven actually be that close, or was he looking into what we would call a mother ship? When God is seen, there will the presence of heaven be. Jacob evidently was looking up a ladder going into a space ship or a ship which today's watchers would call a mother ship which, because of the presence of the Lord, would be heaven.

There are other instances where persons or objects were influenced by what we would call supernatural phenomenon, such as where the Lord has interceded in an event in our life or healing miracles performed by God. We don't discount these acts which will be further witnessed as we develop our faith.

Wings of An Angel

Do angels really have wings. This discussion will enable you to make a comparison of and angel with that of a bird and reach a conclusion that may surprise you.

The most prominent feature of a bird is the breast which constitutes the larger part of the bird. If you will take a look at all birds in general, their main feature is the breast. We've all seen the huge size of the breast of our Thanksgiving turkey. The breast is the main muscle group that powers the wings. Without the huge breast muscles the wings would be powerless to lift the bird into the air. This would be true of anything that flies. An Angel, should he have wings, would have proportionate breast muscles as all birds. This is true of all flying birds.

And how is it we see pictures and references of biblical figures with no huge breast muscles but with large wings. Angels likely do not have wings. They do not need them!. Wings have been shown on angels by early church leaders to give an explanation of how they can move about in the air with no visible means to keep them airborne. Strong's Concordance gives some interesting thoughts about wings:

Hebrew #3671 Kanaph *kaw-nawf'* an edge or an extremity. a wing of a garment or bed clothing. A flap(of the earth), a quarter of a building. a pinnacle, bird, border, corner and feather. overspreading, skirt, sort, uttermost part

The traditional description of a winged angel would violate the laws of nature by being part bird and part human which is impossible. This is one area where we need to use our head and avoid the confusion early church leaders have caused by nothing more than an opinion. They understood not the methods of flight and biology and merely assumed they had wings to explain how angels are able to fly. And, of course, we wonder how one with wings would actually sleep!

The Lord is in no way restricted to our way of thinking and explaining his creations. He is a God of order and works in a more or less natural order of things. He wants us on earth to be also a person of intelligent order. We don't deny the fact that the Lord sometimes moves in mysterious ways They are mysterious to us because we don't understand them.

Some think of the Lord as an ancient old man who has no high technological ideas at all. God created us all, and he knew all about today's modern day world long before we started living on earth. We are talking about the most intelligent Being who has ever been. He has invented and created everything. God brings these things along and prompts mortal men and women to bring them to pass through their earthly inventions. We receive the prompting from God as he declares their need. When the need is present for hydrogen, ionic or fuel cell cars, the Lord will prompt some of us and we will develop the new technology. Edison did not invent the light bulb until the time the Lord declared it. The same goes for everything we experience here on earth. We can not rush things as some would believe. We can only wait until the time is right, and as we progress in our age, the technology increases. Daniel speaks of this in Dan 12:4.

What we have now in our modern day and age is only what God has given us through inventions which were inspired by God.

As one considers a modern day computer there's a sense of wonder and awe! The computer can perform in a matter of minutes and sometimes seconds a series of computations that would take us weeks to do. We look into the box that houses our computer and we see some small green boards, wiring, a few small drives and some electrical fittings. We are overwhelmed by the whole lot. The brain to the computer is the micro-processor; a very small physical part of the overall operation.

God has given this to us. He has computers which would leave our most modern ones in the dust. Don't think for a minute that He is not at the top in technical knowledge.

God has all we have and more. We spoke of Ezekiel's space craft and we know these were around at least 2500 years ago! Why would we think they are not here today. They more than likely come from a different realm here on earth. More and more people are seeing strange craft flying in the sky at great speeds. We cannot dismiss the great number of reported flying craft as hoaxes.

Where do Spirits Go at Death

Religions vary in their belief about what happens to the spirit at death. Does the spirit remain with the body as it lies in the earth and decays or has it gone on to another place where it remains until the time of the end. That the spirit remains with the body is called by some "soul sleeping."

The Bible is quite clear on the subject of the soul at death and we will cover some of the Bible passages that do away with a lot of false thinking about the subject.

Matthew 22:32 states:

"I am the God of Abraham, and the God of Isaac and the God of Jacob? God is not the God of the dead, but of the living."

Another passage in the Bible tells us "the dead know nothing." Of course this is true. However, the spirit is not dead. So, we must assume the spirit does know things, but the body which has been placed in the ground cannot know anything. The body will decay and turn into dust.

Ecclesiastes 12:7 tells us:

"Then shall the dust (body) return to the earth as it was: and the spirit shall return to God who gave it."

Luke 23:43 regarding the thief on the cross stated:

"...and Jesus said unto him, Verily, I say unto thee, Today shalt thou be with me In paradise."

And of course this statement was told the thief on the cross at the time of the sacrifice of Christ on the cross. We go to Strong's Concordance to find out just where paradise is:

Meaning of the word Paradise:

3857 paradisos - par-ad'-i-sos; of oriental or. (comp 6508); a park
i.e. (spec.) an Eden (place of future happiness,
"paradise"): paradise

And this is a direct reference to the spirit heaven where spirits of all who have died reside.

Peter further adds in 1 Peter 3:19-20:

"By which also He went and preached to the spirits in prison;

Which sometime were disobedient, when once the longsuffering of God waited in the days of Noah, while the ark was preparing, wheras few, that is eight souls were saved by water."

Christ spent time in the spirit prison - a place where the spirits reside - to preach to them so they would have the same opportunity as we living on earth who have been taught and given the chance for salvation. Peter further explained in 1 peter 4:6:

"For this cause was the gospel preached also to them that are dead, that they might be judged according to men in the flesh, but live according to God in the spirit."

Christ preached salvation to the spirits of the dead which were from the beginning who had never been offered the atoning power.

There are other passages in the Bible that support the belief that the spirit is alive and aware in a special place awaiting the second advent when Christ returns to the earth to set up his millennial kingdom. There and then they will receive their perfect spiritual body and will dwell with the lord through the thousand year reign and after that forever in the Kingdom of God on Earth.

CHAPTER Ten
Feel Good Doctrines

We are told by Paul in I Thessalonians 5:21 to prove all things:

"Prove all things; hold fast that which is good."

Some of us very carefully listen to what the pastor is saying and likely will notice any deviation from biblical writ as far as we are familiar through study of the Bible. The problem is most will not study the Bible but assume the preacher or teacher is always right in teaching truth and will put complete trust in him. They sometimes say "if it was good enough for my mother and father, it's good enough for me." The pastor could be wrong or mistaken. For this reason Paul has advised and admonished us to prove all things. Lots of ministers teach *Feel Good* doctrine which is pleasing to the congregation but may not be rooted in the scriptures.

The mainline protestant churches - Baptist, Methodist, Presbyterian and others - have, over the years. adopted many non-biblical feel good traditions and imposed them as part of their doctrines. While they are doctrines of the church, they do not necessarily follow the true meanings or teachings of the Bible. Many pastors are knowingly teaching anti Biblical doctrine and traditions.

The Rapture

One of the most prominent subjects of mainstream Protestantism is a belief in a phenomenon called *the rapture;* that Christ will descend from the heavens to near the earth and the elect will rise to meet him in the air. Most churches teach this doctrine and members are quick to believe. They believe this will save them from the tribulation period.

The actual word *rapture* is nowhere to be found in the Bible!

Theologians claim I Thessalonians 4: 16 & 17 as the authority for their rapture:

"For the Lord Himself shall descend from heaven with a shout and with the voice of the archangel, and the trump of God; and the dead in Christ shall rise first.

"Then we which are alive and remain shall be caught up together with them in the clouds to meet the lord in the air; and so shall we ever be with the Lord."

Come Up Hither

Some popular well known evangelists refer to Rev. 4:1 as proof of the rapture:

"After this I looked, and behold, a door was opened in heaven;

and the first voice which I heard *was* as it were a trumpet talking with me; which said, Come up hither, and I will shew thee things which must be hereafter."

This is obviously the angel telling John to come to where he is to receive more revelation regarding the end times and things which must happen prior to and directly after the millennium.

.

The phrase "come up hither" does not constitute a rapture or a gathering back to the Lord.. The phrase is used by many pastors as well as teachers and televangelists to suggest a rapture, which it most emphatically does not. A small child would be able to read and understand what the scriptural meaning implies; yet we have televangelists who are held in high esteem as well as our local pastors and churchmen pushing this theory.

It's very obvious the angel is inviting John to come up to where he is and he would be given a vision pertaining to latter day prophecy.

Left Behind a Work of Fiction

There are many books written on the rapture, including the latecomer fiction about those who were left behind. Many pastors, television ministers and teachers preach this same rapture theory. It's not described in the bible in the manner in which they present it. However, we must agree there will come a time of a gathering when we who are prepared will be gathered back to the Lord after the tribulation period. to meet the Lord; whether it be in the air or spirit, which some interpret as air. Christ will come to the earth and gather his elect from the four corners of the earth and not from the sky (Mark 13:27).

Some televangelists and writers say the landscape will be littered with piles of clothing where those who have been "raptured" have risen in the air. One televangelist remarked about what the astronauts at the space station would think when they see everybody going past the space station as they rise into the air. These are actual comments by well noted evangelists and are approaching mother goose status.

As we analyze I Thessalonians 4:17 above we find some of the terms used can be interpreted differently than written above. The word *cloud* has been used some places in the Bible to mean a multitude as Hebrews 12:1:

"Wherefore seeing we also are compassed about with so great a *cloud* of witnesses."

The word *spirit* is often used for the word air. Then we could have verse seventeen proclaiming:

"Then we which are alive and remain shall be caught up together with them in the multitudes to meet the Lord in the spirit, and so shall we ever be with the Lord."

The phrase "caught up together" merely means we will be grouped together. Caught up does not mean we will go up into the sky.

It's apparent that Jesus did not teach rapture in the four gospels. If one would believe, were the rapture to take place, it would surely be part of His teachings while on earth. Actually, he taught against rapture. Nowhere other than I Thessalonians is this theory even mentioned. Should a rapture take place, surely it would be fully covered as all doctrines of Christ in the Bible. The Bible does not support the rapture theory anywhere. As a matter of fact the prophets of the Old Testament preach of a return to Israel to set up the final assembly of God's Kingdom on earth. They do not mention rising in the sky to meet the Lord in the air.

In the book of Mark, Christ teaches about the final days and events to take place at that time. The elect will be present here on earth when Satan is here. And he will be persecuting the elect (Mark 13:9):

"But take heed to yourselves: for they shall deliver you up to the councils; and in the synagogues ye shall be beaten: and ye shall be brought before rulers and Kings for my sake, for a testimony against them."

Naturally, should there be a rapture, this would never happen. And pay close attention to these words because they were spoken by Christ!

Christ will come in the clouds with great power and glory (Mark 13:24 & 27):

"But in those days, after that tribulation, the sun shall be darkened, and the moon shall not give her light."

"And then shall he send his angels, and shall gather together his elect from the four winds, from the uttermost part of the earth to the uttermost part of heaven."

Take note of the phrase; AFTER THE TRIBULATION, during which time the elect will be tormented. It shall be after this event when Christ shall send his angels to gather his elect from the four corners of the earth. A meeting in the sky is nowhere mentioned. Again, these are words of Christ. We must accept the words of Christ over the traditions of the churches. Televangelists go on television with their own timetable usurping the timing already set up by the Lord. This is wrong and a degrading statement against the words of the Bible!

The whole theme of the rapture taught today is that it provides a way to escape the tribulation. I will not happen according to

Mark 13!

Isaiah also has prophesied about those gathering back to Christ in Isaiah 11:12:

"And he shall set up an ensign for the nations, and shall assemble the outcasts of Israel, and gather together the dispersed of Judah from the four corners of The earth."

Isaiah mentions no meeting in the sky, but a gathering from the four corners of the earth!

Some writings by Paul to the gentile nations are likely for the understanding of those nations only.   If we compare the above quoted scriptures to those of II Thessalonians 2:3 & 4, we can determine Paul was trying to clear up some further misunderstanding regarding the matter and that he had unintentionally misled the Thessalonians:

"Let no man deceive you by any means; for *that day shall not come,* except there shall come a falling away first, and that man of sin be revealed, the son of perdition;

"Who opposeth and exalteth himself above all that is called God, or that is worshipped; So that he as God sitteth in the temple of God, showing himself that he is God."

This plainly tells us, should there be a rapture, it would happen after the tribulation period quoted above. And this alone blows the rapture theory to bits. Rapture churches completely ignore this scripture!

We refer to Webster's dictionary to get a secular definition of the word rapture:

rap'ture (rap'char) *n* ecstatic joy

Again, Webster is giving a very vague definition that cannot be as profound as the popularly described meeting (rapture) in I Thessalonians 4:17. It's obvious there will be a meeting with the Lord as we are told in the gospels and other parts of the bible. It will not be in the air or in the sky as some believe. When the Lord returns to earth, it will be in accordance with the scriptures such as shown in Acts 1:9 thru 11:

"And when He had spoken these things, while they beheld, he was taken up and a cloud received him out of their sight.

"And while they looked steadfastly toward heaven as He went up, behold two men stood by them in white apparel:

"Which also said, Ye men of Galilee, why stand ye staring up into heaven? this same Jesus, which is taken up from you into heaven, shall so come in like manner as ye have seen him go into heaven."

If we believe these scriptures, then we can not believe Jesus will descend almost to earth, but will descend fully to earth in "like manner" as He ascended into heaven. He likely will not stop on the way for some to join him in the sky. A question that lurks in our minds is if we should rise to meet the lord in the sky, where do we go afterward? The scripture says we will ever be with the Lord. Where will the Lord go after the rapture?

Israel to Return to Promised Land

The Bible speaks in many places of a return to our original promised land in Israel. If Jesus is coming to gather his elect, will he come on to earth to set up his earthly kingdom or will he take the elect to heaven first and then come on fully to earth. We have many unanswered questions regarding today's popular theory of rapture. If Jesus comes to gather his elect and

117

they shall "forever be with the Lord" then they must be with the Lord when he sets up his kingdom on earth. Prophets of the Old Testament promise a return of the house of Israel to their original promised land in Palestine. The book of Mark says Jesus will gather his elect from around the world as stated above. The prophet Isaiah speaks of a highway for the remnant of Israel as it was when the Israelites departed Egypt (Isaiah 11:16):

"And there shall be an highway for the remnant of his people, which shall be left, from Assyria; like it was to Israel in the day that he came up out of the land of Egypt."

The remnant of his people left over from Assyria are today's descendants of the Tribes of Israel who were taken captive by Assyria. This indicates the tribes scattered around the world would not be "raptured" as clergy teaches and believes today. Everything will be in natural order and those of the Lost Tribes will travel, on this highway or otherwise, to the land of their original inheritance. Of course we are not talking about a 4-lane interstate road as we would picture in our mind, but of a return route well known to the Lost Tribes of Israel that would lead us to our original home in the Palestinian area.

The book of Revelation describes the timing sequence of the latter days when satan makes his debut on earth in Revelation 13:5, 7 & 8:

"And there was given unto him a mouth speaking great things and blasphemies and power was given him to continue forty and two months.

"And it was given unto him to make war with the saints, and to overcome them; and power was given to him over all kindreds, and tongues and nations.

"And all that dwell upon the earth shall worship him, whose

names are not written in the book of life of the Lamb slain from the foundations of the world."

Satan will come in like a lamb with nice manners, words and flattery and performing miracles and will amaze many. The first half of Satan's time on earth will be for setting up his headquarters in Jerusalem. He will be admired and loved by many. The second period of forty two months will be used to subjugate and make war with the whole world and especially the elect.

Take note of the word "continue" in verse 5 above. Satan has been at work for the first forty two months and he will continue for the final forty two months culminating the full seven year period.

The Last Trump

We can only believe there will be a gathering with the Lord and it will be after the tribulation period on earth when we are changed in the twinkling of an eye as recorded in I Corinthians 15:51-52:

"Behold I shew you a mystery; we shall not all sleep, but we shall all be changed.

"in a moment, in the twinkling of an eye, at the last trump; for the trumpet shall sound and the dead shall be raised incorruptible, and we shall be changed."

A key phrase; "at the last trump" nails down the timing of the our gathering back to Christ. At the last trump Christ will set his feet on earth for the first time since he ascended into heaven after the resurrection. Why would those rise to meet the Lord in the air if they are merely going to turn around and come back to earth? And, who will be the elect at that time?

Many assume those rising to meet the Lord in the air will be taken to heaven for protection from the tribulation. As we have shown above, this cannot be true. Christ says the elect will be gathered from the four corners of thee earth *AFTER THE TRIBULATION* (Mark 13:24 and 27).

The rapture is a very controversial subject which, when discussed, has almost political fallout. Many hold to this theory and get very upset and angry when discussing it. Some arrogantly push their understanding of the rapture while others believe there will not be a rapture. We've all seen the televangelists arrogantly push their rapture theory and they get loud obnoxious and very vocal about the subject. Some of them have written books on the rapture and are selling them to their congregation.

Many think the theory of rapture came from someone who was mentally challenged in the 1830's. However, whatever your beliefs, the subject should be approached calmly while in tune with the scriptures. Whatever your belief about the rapture theory, isn't it proper to take the advice of Paul in I Thessalonians 5:21: "Prove all things."

As we are told above when Christ sets his feet on the Mount of Olives (I Corinthians 15:52), we will all change at that time into a spiritual body that cannot be destroyed. After that time, the elect will be gathered from around the world, and all will see the Lord and the meeting that Paul speaks of may occur. It does not say we will rise in the sky.

Many pastors and believers are obsessed with the rapture theory and rapture becomes a main belief in churches around the world. It's obvious that the rapture theory is taking away the time and effort that should be put into preaching and teaching the real principles of the Bible.

We must conclude the rapture theory is another in a long list of false doctrines the protestants clergy and others are pushing. It absolutely will not happen as rapture theorists would have you believe.

Words spoken by Paul to the Thessalonians can not override the words of Christ as written in the gospel of Mark.

Faith Healers

We have seen televangelists look into a television camera and imply they could see people with afflictions being healed. They usually select a sickness of which there are many, such as cancer and diabetes.

The televangelists likely doesn't see anything but the lens of the TV camera. They are suggesting sicknesses are being healed because of their ministry. Many people around the country have these afflictions and it's true many are being healed. The power of God with help from the doctors are doing the healing. God likely did not give anyone the ability to look into the lens of a camera and see folks being healed. When the televangelist looks into the camera and pronounces healing, he never gives the name or the location of the person being healed because he can't! It's not too long afterward that the ministry will be begging for money. They sell a myriad of CDs, tapes and printed material and suggest you pay with a credit card which is a violation of the laws of usury.
The Bible encourages all of us to avoid usury (Ezekiel 22:12).

It becomes obvious some of these ministries are a family run business designed to make them rich. One would think, should a person be called of God to perform a service, his focus would be on teaching and administering to his own church congregation and not selling books and tapes or CD's by television.

We should never support ministries that treat folks like they don't have a whit of common sense. People are much smarter this day and age than they were 50 or 60 years ago. Remember what the book of Daniel says; "knowledge will increase." Hopefully, it has.

Big Tent Healing

There are several carnival type faith healers who hold a "healing" service in a large auditorium or a tent. They will line people to be healed in a healing order or line so they can approach the "healer." The faith healer will then lay his hands on them and pronounce that they are healed. Those being "healed" will fall backwards and are caught by some assistants and sometimes will demonstrate their new healed body by walking with the faith healer while he proclaims they are healed. We have seen hypnotists perform similar acts on stages before a live audience much as the faith healers do. This they call entertainment.

We have never seen a faith healer restore an arm or leg or heal anyone from a chronic disease. Their healing is more on the line of power such as is used in hypnotic suggestion. During a healing session in Tulsa several years ago where a large group of people were standing in line waiting to be healed, there was a lady with a child suffering from cerebral palsy. When the faith healer got to her, he was perplexed and told the lady she needed to find a miracle worker. He tried unsuccessfully to heal the child and could not heal her at this time and was obviously doubting his own abilities as a faith healer.

This mode of healing is a type of healing that could be conducted by a hypnotic spell. It's called the power of suggestion and sometimes it works until the "spell" wears off.

We would urge anyone who wants to be healed to consult the

bible in James 5:14 & 15:

Obviously, those faith healers and those being healed have not studied the bible. There's a method of healing that is real. It's outlined in plain English in the bible.

"Is any sick among ye? Let him call for the elders of the church; and let them pray over him, anointing him with oil in the name of the Lord:

"And the prayer of the faith shall save the sick and the Lord will raise him up; and if he have committed sins, they shall be forgiven him."

And, of course, James would not mislead anyone. After all, he was a brother to Jesus.

Sowing the Seed of Faith

Many televangelists will urge you to send in your money and it will grow by anywhere from seven to a hundred fold - or more - in return. Their implication is that if you will send in your "seed" money it will grow and eventually reward you with riches. At that rate, your thousand dollars would give you back seven thousand - or more! Should this prove to be true we would likely see thousands of folks standing in line waiting to send their life's savings to the evangelist . Of course the televangelist would like you to send the "seed" money to his ministry. This scheme works well for him, but you're going to lose out in the long run. While he's flitting about the country in his Lear Jet, that you helped buy, you may end up hitchhiking. Jesus did not teach this principle while here with us on earth. Rather he taught the opposite as in Matt. 6:19 & 20:

"Lay not up for yourselves treasures on earth, where moth and rust doth corrupt,

And where thieves break through and steal.

"But lay up for yourselves treasures in heaven, where neither moth nor rust doth corrupt, and where thieves do not break through nor steal."

It's obvious Jesus is inviting us to leave worldly possessions behind and concentrate on the better things because life on earth is temporary and being rich will corrupt us rather than make us richer. Many evangelists today preach and teach for money and not for the sake of their calling. Christianity is not about being rich, but about service to others and obeying the laws of God. While it good to support righteous callings and offer financial assistance, money is not the prominent message of the Bible. Remember, give your donations to your local church.

Divorce and the Church

According to many protestant churches today - including Baptist, Methodist and Pentecostal - divorce is an unpardonable sin. They give no slack for divorced persons whatever the reason. Jesus covered divorce in Matthew 19:8 & 9:

"he said unto them, Moses because of the hardness of your hearts suffered you to put away your wives: but from the beginning it was not so.

"And I say unto you, Whosoever shall put away his wife, except for fornication, and shall marry another, committeth adultery: and whoso marrieth her which is put away doth commit adultery."

And taking a closer look, the phrase "except for fornication," we see this statement tells us that most aren't guilty of committing adultery. Meaning, there is a way for the majority of divorcees to be free from this guilt. Most are divorced because of fornication and unfaithfulness of a spouse. But, this is not the case with which the churches judge. To them all divorcees are the same. The implication is divorced persons are going to wind up in hell. Yet, the Bible tells us all sin will be forgiven except the unpardonable sin of blasphemy against the Holy Spirit. Truth is, a divorced person can repent and be forgiven for any and all sins.

All divorced persons are looked down on by pastors, teachers and members of the various churches. And, of course, this causes gossip by the do-gooders which are determined to destroy any union with the divorced. In some cases, the divorced becomes an outsider and eventually leaves the church.

Many divorced members of the congregation have been damaged psychologically and emotionally by some meaningless doctrines of the church and members, with a self imposed practice of malicious gossip designed to destroy others. Some within the church have committed more grievous sins than divorce. Many pastors are guilty of more serious sins and have the gall to get in front of the congregation and condemn others. According to Jesus Christ, divorce can and will be forgiven per Matt. 12:31:

"Wherefore I say unto you, all manner of sin and blasphemy shall be forgiven unto men: but the blasphemy *against* the *Holy* Ghost shall not be forgiven unto men."

Is divorce really an unpardonable sin? Of course not. Any sin can be forgiven except the one mentioned above of blaspheming the Holy Spirit.

God does not say the divorced person cannot be forgiven. If you are divorced, repent and go on with your life. Many have done worse than you. Some of them stand at the pulpit!

Once Saved-Always Saved

Another doctrine of some churches is the belief "Once Saved, Always Saved." There are sins leading to death as spoken by John (1 John 4:16) One can fall away from God once he has obtained salvation. While it's true, once you are saved, you don't have to be baptized again and as long as you truly repent you will stay saved. Rather than being baptized again, you would merely repent of all sins. We can fall away from the grace of God through sin as explained in Peter 2:21:

"For it had been better for them not to have known the way of righteousness, than after they have known it, to turn from the holy commandments delivered unto them."

Also, we are told in Philippians 2:12; "...work out your own salvation with fear and trembling"

Snake Handling

America is a continent with many snakes. Some of them are poisonous while others such as the blacksnake are not. All poisonous snakes are to be avoided. We are told by authorities which ones to avoid which, if bittern, could cause death or very severe sickness. Snake handling at churches, while not all that prominent, are practiced in some areas of the country and are conducted in very unsafe conditions. There's no protection for congregations that attend these meetings. Anyone could accidentally get bitten.

The apostles of Christ were given protection as the Lord had promised as they traveled throughout the land with the good news Christ had commissioned them to teach. They were shipwrecked and sought after by their enemies, and at one time, they experienced an incident of snakebite while they were shipwrecked on an island called Melita. They were preparing for encampment and getting a fire built to be warmed from the cold, rain and wind (Acts 28: 1-6):

"And when they were escaped, then they knew the island was called Mel'-i-ta.

"And the barbarous people shewed us no little kindness for they kindled a fire, and received us everyone, because of the present rain, and because of the cold.

"And when Paul had gathered a bundle of sticks, and laid them on the fire, there came a viper out of the heat, fastened on his hand.

"And when the barbarians saw the *venomous* beast hang on his hand, they said among themselves, no doubt this man is a murderer, whom though he has escaped the sea, yet vengeance suffered him not to live.

"And he shook off the beast into the fire, and felt no harm.

"Howbeit, they looked when he should have swollen, of fallen down dead suddenly; but after they had looked a great while, and saw no harm come to him, they changed their minds, and said that he was a god."

This protection was given to the apostles and few others because the venom from a serpent would surely kill others. Some religions today - called snake handlers - have taken this example of how they should prove their trust in God. They have completely misunderstood the words of the Bible. The message in Mark 16:14-20 following the resurrection of the Lord who appeared to them as they sat at meat:

"Afterwards he appeared to the eleven as they sat at meat, and upbraided them with their unbelief and hardness of heart, because they believed not them which had seen Him after he was risen.

"And he said unto Him, Go *ye* into all the world, and preach the gospel to every creature.

"He that believeth and is baptized shall be saved; but he that believeth not shall be damned.

"And these signs shall follow them that believe; In My name they shall cast out devils; they shall speak with new tongues.

"They shall take up serpents; and if they drink any deadly thing, it shall not hurt them; they shall lay hands on the sick, and they shall recover."

Poisonous Snakes will Bite

It is obvious that anyone grabbing a snake is in danger of being bitten and this has been proven through snakebite at worship services. As you recall the incident above where Paul was bitten, he did not deliberately handle the snake as a show, but through the protection of God that he was promised that he could "take up serpents." He was in the service of God at the time and the snake had no effect on him.

Divine Protection Promised

The subject here is the protection you likely will have as you travel about preaching the word of God and obviously is not valid as you deliberately handle a serpent to prove your own faith. When you do this, you are tempting God and He does not condone that.

Today, we have several groups in the backwoods of Tennessee, West Virginia and Kentucky that still practice this belief. They go to the forests and capture rattlesnakes and copperheads and bring them to a snake handling service and some have been bitten and died from the venom. They bring prepared strychnine to the services for those who want to show their faith to drink thus they are poisoned and some also die from this.

There are many more strange adopted doctrines by today's Christian churches which have no truth in the word of God. We are told in scripture to "prove all things" and to "test the spirits" we should attune our beliefs to those that are known to be real scriptural writings of the Bible.

The acts listed above such as taking up serpents, speaking with new tongues, casting out devils and healing were not given to the apostles of Christ (or anyone else) to provide entertainment such as a sideshow. Many attend church which provide these acts out of curiosity and gain no saving knowledge by this.

Talking in Tongues

Talking in an unknown tongue has become a practice of the charismatic churches in that they will spontaneously speak without understanding (or others understanding) what they are saying. Both men and women take part in this practice and began to converse one to another, yet they understand not what they are saying. They will tell you they don't know what they are saying because, they say, it is the Holy Ghost that is speaking through them. This practice is taken from Acts 2:1-4;

"And when the day of Pentecost was fully come, they were of one accord in one place.

"And suddenly there came a sound from heaven as of a rushing mighty wind, and it filled the house where they were sitting.

"And there appeared unto them cloven tongues like as of fire, and it sat upon each of them.

"And they were all filled with the Holy Ghost, and began to speak with other tongues, as the spirit gave them utterance.

Continuing in Acts 2:5-8, we find the language spoken was not an unknown tongue, but was fully understood by all:

"And there were dwelling at Jerusalem Jews, devout men, out of every nation under heaven.

"Now when this was noised abroad, the multitude came together, and were confounded, because that every man heard them speak in his own language.

"And they were all amazed and marveled, saying one to another, Behold are not all which speak Galileans?

"And how hear we every man in our own tongue , wherein we were born?"

There was no unknown mysterious tongue spoken at the day of Pentecost in the upper room as the language of every one in the room sounded like his very own language where he was born.

Going further into I Corinthians 14:2:

"For he that speaketh in an *unknown* tongue, speaketh not unto men, but unto God: for no man understandeth *him;* howbeit in the spirit he speaketh mysteries.

We need only put the phrase *"unknown* tongue" into today's English we would better understand the phrase is saying "foreign language." Thus, we fully understand the phrase.

All throughout the Bible Italicized words are used. They are not part of the original manuscript but they were put there by the translators of the Bible to make it fully understandable.

Thus the verse would read:

"For he that speaks in an foreign language, speaks not unto men, but unto God; for no man can understand him; howbeit in the spirit he speaks mysteries.

This merely means when you speak in a foreign language, nobody will be able to understand you and only you will be able to understand and it would be mysterious to all except God and you or anyone else who could speak that language.

When an evangelist goes to a foreign country to preach he must take an interpreter with him, otherwise only the interpreter and God would know what he speaks.

Paul further explains in I Corinthians 15: 27 & 28:

"If any man speak in an *unknown* tongue, let it be by two, or at the most, *by* three And *that* by course; and let one interpret.

"But if there be no interpreter, let him keep his silence in the church; and let him speak to himself, and to God.

And. of course, God understands all languages of the world. He's the one that confounded the languages at the tower of Babel!

CHAPTER Eleven
Biblical Food Laws for Good Health

The biblical laws for good health are given in Leviticus 11 and outlines all animals fit for human consumption as given in Leviticus 11:1-8:

"And the Lord spoke to Moses and to Aaron, saying unto them,

"Speak unto the children of Israel, saying. These *are* the beasts which ye shall eat among all the beasts that *are* on the earth.

"Whatsoever parteth the hoof, and is clovenfooted, *and* cheweth the cud, among the beasts, that shall ye eat.

"Nevertheless these shall *ye* not eat of them that chew the cud, or of them that divide the hoof: as the camel, because he cheweth the cud, but divideth not the hoof; he is unclean unto you.

"And the coney, because he cheweth the cud, but divideth not he hoof; he *is* unclean unto you.

"And the hare, because he cheweth the cud, but divideth not the hoof; he *is* unclean unto you.

"And the swine, though he divideth the hoof, and be cloven-footed, yet he cheweth not the cud; he *is* unclean unto you.

"Of their flesh shall *ye* not eat, and their carcass shall *ye* not touch; they *are* unclean to you."

A coney mentioned above is nothing more than a rock rabbit - the same as a hare as far as restrictions go. Thus, above we have described land animals that may be consumed by man. We now go to Leviticus 11:9-12 listing clean fish and water life that may be consumed:

"These shall *ye* eat of all that *are* in the waters: whatsoever hath fins and scales in the waters, in the seas, and in the rivers, them shall *ye* eat.

"And all that have not fins and scales in the seas, and in the rivers, of all that move in the waters, and any living thing which *is* in the waters, they *shall be* an abomination unto you:

"They shall be even an abomination unto you; ye shall not eat of their flesh, but ye shall have their carcases in abomination.

"Whatsoever hath no fins nor scales in the waters, that shall be an abomination unto you."

You may consume any fish of the sea that has scales and fins. Others not mentioned such as crab, lobster, catfish, oysters, squid, turtles, octopus and others without scales nor fins is surely not healthy! Catfish is a bottom feeder and does not have scales. Whether it's farm raised catfish or river caught, it is still not approved for human consumption.

As to fowl and clean birds we may safely eat are named in Leviticus 11:13-23:

"And these *are they which ye* shall have in abomination among the fowls; They shall not be eaten, they *are* an abomination; the eagle, and the suffrage, and the osprey,

"And the vulture, and the kite after his kind.

"Every raven after his kind;

"And the owl, and the night hawk, and the cuckoo, and the hawk after his kind,

"And the little owl, and the cormorant, and the great owl,

"And the swan, and the pelican, and the gier eagle,

"And the stork, the heron after her kind, and the lapwing, and the bat.

"All fowls that creep, going upon *all four shall be* an abomination unto you.

"Yet these may ye eat of every flying creeping thing that goeth upon *all* four, which have legs above their feet, to leap withal upon the earth;

"*Even* these of them ye may eat; the locust after his kind, and the bald locust after his kind, and the beetle after his kind, and the grasshopper after his kind.
"But all *other* flying creeping things, which have four feet, *shall* be an abomination unto you.

"These also *shall* be unclean unto you among the creeping things that creep Upon the earth; the weasel, and the mouse, and the tortoise after his kind.

"And the ferret, and the chameleon, and the lizard, and the snail, and the mole.

"These are *unclean* to you among all that creep; whosoever doth touch them, when they be dead, shall be unclean until the even."

So, there's no doubt God wanted us to be healthy by abstention from things that would be harmful. Most people violate the above, especially the eating of swine flesh which we would classify as any pork in any form.

There are those who try to rationalize eating forbidden meat by stating there was no refrigeration in Moses' time thus the meat would spoil or rot. This is false thinking as animals mentioned as forbidden food are clearly identified as scavengers that eat all manner of scum from the earth.

We present this testimonial from a close dear friend who has had first hand experience regarding the proper food to repair and continue your life:

"Having completed recovery from a heart operation which resulted in and   corrected five blockages in the heart and requiring four grafts, I resolved to take measures to insure this would never happen again. My first recourse was to instill a diet that would eliminate any build up of fats in my body. In doing so, several things came to mind which made very good sense.

"Recalling my personal history regarding my health, and eating disorders, which in the past were never thought to be a problem, but today glares back at me as a horrible threat to my life.

136

"Several years ago, Eastern Kentucky was declared a medical disaster area scoring twenty per cent above the national average in the number of deaths from heart attacks, diabetes, cancer, Parkinson's, Alzheimers and other major diseases that cause death.

"Eastern Kentucky is not the culprit as many live here to a ripe old age. Rather it's the lifestyle and dietary habits of Eastern Kentucky that have killed and crippled many residents of this eastern part of a great state.

"Growing up in Eastern Kentucky, one cannot escape the fact that eating is one of the greatest enjoyments of life, especially when folks gather to celebrate an event. We only have to visit a doctor's office to see the many grossly overweight and sickly folks. I can recall the lifestyles in Eastern Kentucky that was prevalent in my own family. We would butcher hogs every year as that was the norm in preparation of the winter protein storage package. Our concentration was on hog killing time. During the winter months we would have all manner of pork prepared as listed:

Salt Pork	Baby Back Ribs
Pork Roasts	Pork Liver
Liverwurst	Ham
Smoked Bacon	Fatback
Lunch Meats	Weiners
Sausages	Pork Rinds

"Salt pork, alone fried, or used as a seasoning and a myriad of foods flavored with pork drippings was in dominance. Lard was used to cook all foods including desserts and the pie crusts and cakes.

"A 50# can of Lard was stored in the kitchen for easy access. Pork fat has been used as a staple. I've seen a few old timers dip cornbread and biscuits in the fat and slurp away. The ladies used it in cakes, cornbread, biscuits, etc.

"This was my lifestyle and eating regimen as I grew up in Eastern Kentucky and later until I reached the age of 69 at which point my arteries were clogged with fats; a heart bypass was next!

"Since the bypass operation, pork in any size, shape or form has been eliminated from my diet (as are any of the biblically banned foods). How did we become such lovers of pork? Obviously, according to the old adage; pork is a heart attack just waiting to happen!"

We wonder why the medical authorities didn't see this problem long ago and encourage folks to eliminate pork and other harmful meats from their diet. The Lord surely advised us against these harmful meats. Pork will never be eliminated from today's society because it's a major money business to grocers, restaurants and others. We will see it displayed in all stores that sell meat.

It's obvious some animals were created to be the scavengers where they play a very useful role as this is their purpose. We can surely identify these animals. Chief among the unclean animals is the swine (hog) which is called an abomination by the lord and is placed in lowly status. They are called an abomination throughout the bible. A pig will eat anything in it's path including rotted meat and even poisonous snakes. We should hold the swine in the same regard as we would a buzzard or any animal or bird that eats rotted flesh such as road kill. All scavengers are filthy and should be avoided and as the Bible tells us do not even touch these animals.

Most religious leaders of today's Christian churches tell us pork or swine is good for human consumption. They are wrong! God never made any changes in the animals he created between the time of the Old Testament and today. Ministers have recited scriptures from the New Testament to try to prove unclean animals are biblically accepted for your body:

Acts 10:15-15 "...Rise Peter; kill and eat."

This scripture refers to the event when the Lord was preparing Peter to accept the gentile, Cornelius, to be baptized into the church. Until this time, gentiles were considered unclean and not allowed to be members of the Christian faith. The gospel of Christ was to be given to the House of Israel first as recorded in Matt. 10:5-6. And then was to be given to the gentiles. Note: Peter replied that he had never eaten any unclean creature. Do we now assume he could eat any manner of creature that moves upon the earth? Rather, God was telling Peter that gentiles were to be accepted into the church. And we should not assume Peter could partake of unclean animals. They were declared unclean in Leviticus and that fact remains to this day.

As to partaking of clean and unclean animals and proper day for worship, Paul told the Colossian believers in Colossians 2:16:

"Let no man therefore judge you in meat or in drink..."

Paul is addressing the Colossian saints who belong to a nation of gentiles. Most gentiles partake of unclean animals. The saints in this region were warned to allow no man to judge them because they have stopped eating unclean animals as advised in Leviticus. This is scriptural advice to keep us healthy rather than an OK to partake of unclean animals. We must remember during this time the scriptures were the Old Testament as the New Testament had not yet been written. Most biblical teaching came from the Old Testament Only the blood sacrifices were taken away by the sacrifice of Christ. Health laws were not done away with but are the same today as they were in the Old Testament. As one pastor said; "you may eat pork and still go to heaven, but you may get there faster than you had planned."

Clean animals are vegetarians and fit to eat. You would be better of eating fish (as described in Leviticus), beef, lamb chops, poultry and other clean creatures.

Other Harmful Elements Not mentioned in Leviticus

There are many things we partake of that is harmful to our body. The list is almost endless and we will cover some of the worst of these. You are responsible for your good health and should carefully examine what you take into your body. You are responsible for what you eat. If it's not good, do not consume it.

Cigarettes were never mentioned in the biblical food laws, but common sense will tell you this is one of the most dangerous and unhealthy product in use today. It is an increasing addiction to those who start young and grow older. Cigarette smoking depletes the body of oxygen which is needed with every muscle and organ in the body.

The tobacco industry is aware of this and has been known to put additive substances in the tobacco to make one even more addicted. Tobacco, whether smoked in cigarette form or in a pipe or cigar (supposedly cigar smokers don't inhale) is very harmful to your health. Chewing tobacco or snuff is also addictive and devastating to the health.

Substances introduced in our lifetime is very harmful and you are consuming vile substances into your system that is contrary to good health. Inhaling cigarette smoke into your lungs not only causes lung cancer, but many sicknesses including heart diseases, blood pressure problems and who knows what. The oxygen destroying factor is what causes so much cancer and other problems all over the body.

We would advise all against taking anything into your body that could be harmful and damage organs or muscles, or any other parts of you body. Many medicines have been introduced that are harmful and you are to be wary of what the doctors prescribe for whatever is ailing you. We've seen some drugs taken from the market recently because they have caused heart attacks, strokes and death.

There's a disclaimer with all medicines which outlines the possible side effects of a particular medicine. Some list heart attack, stroke, depression and even death as side effects. One would be foolish indeed for treating his disease with a "medicine" that could cause strokes, death or heart attacks! Be not afraid of doctors, after all, they are in your employ. You are paying them! The list of side effects is very long and is designed to protect the drug companies and doctors against being sued for malpractice. Remember, some doctors deliberately murder unborn babies under the name of abortion. In our day and age, we should be very wary of those who could make you sick for life or kill you with their medicine. Doctors kill more than half a million persons per year with improper drugs and their treatment as well as performing other irresponsible acts to include abortion!

Organ donors sounds like a good thing to many of us. We must remember, your organs to be donated should be after your death. This is not always the case. A doctor who would perform an abortion would not be beyond seeking a premature death organ if the money is sufficient. Think about this one folks!

CHAPTER Twelve
We Lived in a Pre-Earth Age

God has revealed a previous earth age when He gave Jeremiah his commission to perform and oversee the destruction and captivity of the Kingdom of Judah. We read In Jeremiah 1:4-5:

"Then the word of the Lord came unto me saying,

"Before I formed thee in the belly, I knew thee; And before thou camest forth out of the womb I sanctified thee, *and* I ordained thee a prophet unto the nations."

Thus, God knew Jeremiah and before this present earth age. So, we know he had a pre-earth age existence. We are not talking about reincarnation, but about a previous earth age where Jeremiah existed in a spiritual body and was known by God and given his commission before being born into a mortal body. Such was the way we all were before being born into our mortal body. We all existed in the pre earth age and were given our callings and gifts which would be with us through all eternity should we choose to obey our God who created the earth.

The bible speaks in Genesis 1:1 thusly:

"In the beginning, God created the heaven and the earth"

The second verse reads:

"And the earth was without form, and void; and darkness *was* upon the face of the deep. And the spirit of God moved upon the face of the waters."

We can assume there was a separation between the first and second verses in Genesis of many thousands and likely millions of years.   Also, we must know for certain when God created the earth, it was perfect. Man occasionally does shoddy work but God's work is perfect.

There's evidence the word "was" can be interpreted as "became" since the word is not in the concordance but appears so many times in the bible. The verse would be; "…and the earth became without form…" When God created the earth, it was perfect, but became void and without form.

As you read the words of the Lord when he blessed Adam and Eve in Genesis 1:28:

"And God blessed them, and God said unto them, Be fruitful, and multiply and replenish the earth…."

To replenish means to refill that which has been used up or is no longer there. Thus God is telling Adam and Eve to repopulate the earth which at this time was empty, or void of any other human beings.

The apostle, Paul also speaks of our pre earthly existence in Ephesians 1:4:

"According as he hath chosen us in him before the foundations of the world That we should be holy and without blame before Him in love."

God has chosen us all, and not only the Ephesians, before the foundations of the world to be holy and without blame before him in love. Paul gave this message to the Ephesians; that they were predestined to be of the adoption into the elect according to the pleasures and the will of Christ. So, we have scriptural proof we lived in the spirit on earth before we were born!

Archaeologists, Paleontologists and scholars have discovered large bones and relics of the past that are not present in our earth age, but relics from the first earth age. Historians and clergy have puzzled over this phenomenon for centuries. There were dinosaurs and their kin in the first earth age as bones and relics have shown. One need only visit a Natural History Museum to see some of the previous earth age animal skeletons displayed including the wooly mammoth, the saber tooth tiger and many others including the dinosaurs. Today's scientists claim these animals roamed the earth 10,000 year ago.

So, it's evident we had a pre-earthly existence. The prehistoric animals whose bones are being discovered and assembled into skeletons today are prehistoric as they were animals of the first earth age.

Twin Sons of Isaac

We are familiar with the twin sons of Isaac named Jacob and Esau. They were surely enemies at their time of conception as we read in Genesis 25:21-26:

"And Isaac intreated the Lord for his wife, because she was barren; and the Lord was intreated of him, and Rebekah, his wife conceived.

"And the children struggled together within her, and she said, if *it* be so, why *am* I thus? And she went to enquire of the Lord.

"And the Lord said unto her, Two nations *are* in thy womb, and two manner of people shall be separated from thy bowels; and *the one* people shall be stronger than *the other* people; and the elder shall serve the younger.

"And when her day to be delivered were fulfilled, behold, *there were* twins in her womb.

"And the first came out red, all over like a hairy garment; and they called his name Esau.

"And after that came his brother out, and his hand took hold on Esau's heel; and his name was called Jacob: and Isaac *was* threescore years old when she bare them."

The name, Jacob, in the Hebrew is translated as "heel grabber" or "supplanter." Jacob obviously was to be the firstborn so he could attain the birthright, but Esau and Jacob fought in the womb of Rebekah and Esau prevailed. He became the first-born but later lost his birthright to Jacob Genesis 25:27-34).

"And the boys grew: and Esau was a cunning hunter, a man of the field; and Jacob *was* a plain man, dwelling in tents.

"And Isaac loved Esau, because he did eat of *his* venison: but Rebekah loved Jacob.

"And Jacob sod pottage: and Esau came from the field, and he *was* Faint:

"And Esau said to Jacob, Feed me, I pray thee, with that same red *pottage;* for I *am* faint: therefore was his name called Edom.

"And Jacob said, Sell me this day thy Birthright.

"And Esau said, Behold, I *am* at the point to die: and what profit shall this birthright do to me?

"And Jacob said, Swear to me this day; and he sware unto him: and he sold his birthright unto Jacob.

"Then Jacob gave Esau bread and pottage of lentils; and he rose up, and went his way: Thus Esau despised *his* birthright."

Scripture goes on to say, in Genesis 27, that Jacob, by devious means, took the blessings that would normally go to the first son of Isaac. Jacob eventually became the patriarch Israel; indeed his name was changed to Israel by the Lord.

Rebekah was told by an the Lord that two nations were in her womb. We know Jacob and his descendents became the nation of Israel and previous to this we have identified today's Israel as America and the Commonwealth of Britain. We ask: who was the nation that Esau was to become.

The main identifying factor of Esau is that he was "red, all over like a hairy garment." Also the soup Jacob gave Esau was a red pottage. The meaning of Edom is Red. Esau's descendents would become the Edomites and Idumea and Obed--

Edom; and finally Russia! The two great nations who were in Rebekah's womb became America and Russia!

We have identified the invading forces of Russia as Gog and Magog who are identified as Edom. Russia, traditionally, was known as the red nation as was Communist China. The communists were known as "Reds" by all free nations (thus the identifying sign of Edom is used to identify the "Russian Reds). Let's not forget the Red pottage mentioned above that Jacob used to buy the birthright from Esau. The national soup of Russia is a Red pottage called Borsch. Edom also is identified in the book of Obadiah. Russia has always compared herself to America as Obadiah 1:4 explains:

"Though thou exalt *thyself* as the eagle, and though thou set thy nest among the Stars thence will I bring thee down, saith the Lord.

America is the eagle spoken of by this verse. The Eagle is the national symbol of this great nation and is identified other places in the bible just as Esau was identified as Edom because he was Red all over. Esau was very bully and threatened that he would kill Jacob for taking his birthright and blessings. Likewise, Russia has always been a bully nation. The democracy Russia talks of today is likely not in existence. Still, they rely upon America for help in keeping their food pantry supplied.

The Lord does not favor Russia in any way as is evidenced by their inability to succeed in their atheistic society. Russia has been bullish since they have been formed as a nation and their leaders have killed off any opposition to their form of government. Having given up communizing and saying they have adopted a democratic government, their leadership still is communistic. The curses on Russia's forefathers have continued as the Lord would have, although not a single citizen of

Russia, with Christian characteristics would be denied salvation, God has made a direct definite statement concerning Esau which is today's Russia as shown in Malachi 1:1-3:

"The burden of the word of the Lord to Israel by Mal'-a-chi.

"I have loved you, saith the Lord. Yet ye say, Wherein hast thou loved us? Was not Esau Jacob's brother? Saith the Lord: yet I loved Jacob.

"And I hated Esau, and laid his mountains and heritage waste for the dragons of the wilderness."

Obviously, Esau did not honor his own heritage even before he was born. But Jacob, who is today's nations of Israel, was very honorable to their heritage and were and still are favored by God.

CHAPTER Thirteen
Transgressions of Our Leaders

Most of our leaders, Kings, and prophets had trouble honoring their heritage and the gifts given by our Creator. We can look at a list of some of our past leaders who have gotten caught up in the enticement of satan and fallen into sinful acts as follows:

****

- Jacob who disguised himself as Esau and stole the birthright blessings (Gen. 27:18-29):

"And he came unto his father , and said, My father: and he said, Here *am* I; who *art* thou, my son?

"And Jacob said unto his father, I *am* Esau thy firstborn; I have done according as thou badest me; arise, I pray thee, sit and eat of my venison, that thy soul may bless me.

"And Isaac said unto his son, How *is it* that thou has found it so quickly, my son? And he said, Because the Lord thy God brought *it* to me.

"And Isaac said unto Jacob, Come near, I pray thee, that I may feel thee, my son, whether thou *be* my very son Esau or not.

"And Jacob went near unto Isaac his father; and he felt him, and said, The voice is Jacob's voice, but the hands are the hands of Esau."

Previous to this, Rebekah and Jacob conspired to fool Isaac because he was old and on his death bed and was almost blind. Rebekah, the wife of Isaac, had favored Jacob to receive the blessing of the birthright. Jacob had previously bought the birthright from Esau for a bowl of red soup. So, Jacob continued showing Isaac his arms and showing by the smell of the woods that he was Esau and Isaac gave him the birthright blessing as shown:

"Therefore God, give thee of the dew of heaven, and the fatness of the earth, plenty of corn and wine;

"Let people serve thee, and nations bow down to thee; be lord over thy brethren, and let thy mother's sons bow down to thee; cursed *be* every one that curseth Thee, and blessed *be* he that blesseth thee."

Actually, Jacob likely was destined to be the birthright holder and own the blessings of the birthright because this was his calling prior to his being born as Jeremiah was called.

****

- Reuben who defiled his father's bed (Gen 48:3-4):

"Reuben, thou art my firstborn, my might, and the beginning of my strength, The excellency of dignity, and the excellency of power.

"Unstable as water, thou shall not excell, because thou wentest up to thy Father's bed; then defiledst thou *it*; he went up to my couch."

Reuben defiled Jacobs couch by having an affair with Jacobs maiden, Bilah.

****

- Judah who had incestuous relations with his daughter in law (Gen. 38:1)

"Then said Judah to Tamar his daughter in law, Remain a widow at thy father's House, till She'-lah my son be grown; for he said, peradventure he die also, as his brethren *did*. And Tamat went and dwelt in her father's house.

Tamar was married previously to Judah's two sons, Er and Onan in succession and they died for the Lord slew them because they were wicked in the sight of the Lord. Tamar also was promised a third son of Judah whose name was She'-lah. She was to wait until She'-lah became of age to be married. She'-lah did not marry Tamar and she plotted and tricked Judah into to fathering her two sons, Pharez and Zara. We have related these events more fully in chapter 3 of this book.

****

- Moses who murdered an Egyptian who was mistreating Israelites (Ex. 2:11-12):

"And it came to pass in those days, when Moses was grown, that he went out unto his brethren, and looked on their burdens: and he spied an Egyptian smiting An Hebrew, one of his brethren.

"And he looked this way and that way, and when he saw that *there was* no man, he slew the Egyptian, and hid him in the sand."

Following this event when Pharaoh heard about this, he sought to slay Moses and he had to flee for his life, and went into the country of Midian and dwelt with Jethro who was descended from Midian, a son of Abraham and Keturah. Moses married one of Jethro's daughters.

****

- David who committed adultery with Uriah's wife and later ordered Uriah to be killed so he could take his wife (II Samuel 12):

Nathan, the prophet came to King David and related a parable about a man and his family who had a pet lamb. There were two men in the town and one was very rich and had many flocks including lambs. The poor man had only the one lamb which he and his family cherished very much as they had bought it while very young and raised it as one of their family and treated it as one of them.

The rich man was preparing to receive a traveler and wanted to make a feast for him. He did not want to use of his own flock and took the poor man's lamb.

David's anger was greatly kindled against the rich man who took the poor man's lamb and told Nathan the man that did this thing should surely die and he should restore the lamb four-fold!

And Nathan said to King David, You are that man, meaning the acts you have performed against Uriah are equal to the rich man who took the poor man's lamb!

The King h saw Bathsheba, Uriah's wife, taking a bath and in-quired of her for she was very beautiful to look upon, and he sent for her to come to him. He lay with her and she con-ceived. David desired her very much and he conspired to send Uriah into battle where he was sure to be killed and he eventu-ally was killed. David took Bathsheba to wife.

The Lord reminded David of all the things he had given him and the honor he gave him in becoming the king of Israel and Judah, pronounced much punishment unto King David and that he would live under the sword the remainder of his life.

The Lord put the sin from David and he continued on as the King of Israel (II Samuel 12:13):

"And David said unto Nathan, I have sinned against the Lord. And Nathan said unto David, the Lord also hath put away thy sin; thou shalt not die."

As we read on into II Samuel, we find David paid a great price for the sins he had Committed. he did not die at the time, but the Lord took away many of his possessions Including his wives and took his child from the union with Uriah's wife, Bathsheba.

****

- Solomon who after being made rich and wise by God turned to idol worship(I Kings 11:1-6):

"But king Solomon loved many strange women, together with the daughter of Pharaoh, women of the Moabites, Ammonites, Edomites, Zidonianites and Hittites;

"Of the nations *concerning* which the Lord said unto the children of Israel, Ye shall not go in to them, neither shall they come in unto you: *for* surely they will turn away your heart after their gods: Solomon clave unto these in love.

"And he had seven hundred wives, princesses, and three hundred concubines; and his wives turned away his heart.

"For it came to pass, when Solomon was old, *that* his wives turned away his heart after other gods: his heart was not perfect with the Lord his God, as *was* the heart of David his father.

"For Solomon went after Ashtoreth the goddess of the Zidonians , and after Milcom the abomination of the Ammonites.

"And Solomon did evil in the sight of the Lord, and went not fully after the Lord as *did* David his father."

****

- Paul who persecuted Christians (Acts 7:58-60 and 8:1-3): Regarding Stephen whom the zealots had stoned to death with his raiment at the feet of Saul who later became Paul.

"And cast *him* out of the city, and stoned *him:* and the witnesses laid their clothes at a young man's feet, whose name was Saul.

"And they stoned Stephen, calling upon *God,* and saying, Lord Jesus, receive my spirit.

"And he kneeled down, and cried with a loud voice, Lord, lay not this sin to their charge. And when he had said this, he fell asleep."

"And Saul was concenting unto his death. And at that time there was a great persecution against the church which was at Jerusalem; and they were all scattered abroad throughout the regions of Judea and Samaria, except the apostles.

"And devout men carried Stephen *to his burial* and made great lamentations over him.

"As for Saul, he made havoc of the church, entering into every house, and haling men and women committed *them* to prison."

And we know this same Saul was struck blind on the way to Damascus and later became Paul, an apostle of Jesus and eventually wrote many of the letters of the New Testament.

As we read on into II Samuel, we find David paid a great price for the sins he had committed. He did not die at the time, but the lord took away many of his possessions including his wives and took his child form the union with Uriah's wife, Bathsheba.

We must remember, we were given our callings in the first earth age and as we have reported previously, all callings and blessings are without repentance! What the Lord has given us to do will be carried out to the fullest. David continued as

King of Israel although he was guilty of adultery and murder. Also, the atoning sacrifice of Christ for forgiveness was not in effect at the time of the kings and prophets of the Old Testament, but after the death of our Lord who gave this gift at the time.

While Christ was entombed for three days and three nights He went into the spirits that were in the spiritual prison to preach to them the new covenant. As Peter explained it in I Peter 3:19-20:

"By which also he went and preached unto the spirits in prison;

"which sometime were disobedient, when once the longsuffering of God waited in the days of Noah, while the ark was a preparing, whereas few, that is, eight souls were saved by the waters."

Continuing in I peter 4:6:

"For this cause was the gospel preached also to them that are dead, that they might be judged according to men in the flesh, but live according to God in the spirit."

God, through his magnificent grace has made the atonement and forgiveness freely to all who live today and during the time of Noah.

All who sinned before the time of Christ were given an opportunity to hear the gospel of Christ and repent as explained by Paul. The sacrifice on the cross covered sins by David, Solomon and others who lived before the time of Christ.

CHAPTER Fourteen
Today's Televangelists

The Bible speaks of the Latter Days or the time of the end, and we can only conclude we are in the latter days at this present time and those events prophesied for the time of the end have been and will continue to come to pass as ancient prophets have promised.

We obviously are in the time spoken of by Amos 8:11-12 which proclaims:

"Behold, the days come, saith the Lord God, that I will send a famine in the land, not a famine of bread, nor a thirst for water, but a hearing of the word of the Lord:

"And they shall wander from sea to sea, and from the north even to the east, they shall run to and fro to seek the word of the Lord, and shall not find it.

159

The truths of the Bible have been suppressed by many Christian denominations and others in order to make way for their own doctrines which are not necessarily Biblical. We talked about the "feel good" doctrines which have very little relationship to the Bible and other non Biblical traditions which have been introduced into almost all churches. This is evident with today's movement to pollute our beliefs with all manner of secular mores this nation has piled upon us such as abortion, homosexuality, pornography, removal of emblems of biblical tenets, such as The Ten Commandments, from our land, and the attempted removal of our national motto: "In God We Trust," which is imprinted on our coinage as well as documents of our nation. When we no longer trust in God, we will no longer reap the blessings of God. We will become a downtrodden nation. This is no secret as it is prophesied throughout the Bible and specifically addressed to the nation of Israel - Ancient Israel as well as today's Israel who are descendants of one of the 12 tribes of Israel called The Lost Tribes of Israel.

As we have shown in previous pages of this book, Israel is alive and well on this earth and present in all nations (even the heathen nations). They today number in the hundreds of millions. Even they, for the most part, don't know who they are as this has been ignored by clerics, historians, researchers and others who are not able to discern the signs and characteristics of Israel. The location of the lost tribes of Israel has been discussed by secular television investigators who have located them in some nations in the middle east areas and Africa. They don't mention the obvious locations: Great Britain and America, who exactly characterize with the latter day descriptions of Israel. Great Britain and America are the two greatest nations that ever has existed. They are not mentioned in scripture by name, but their characteristics are there and they describe these two great nations exactly!

Televangelism has become prominent in these latter days as it has hatched out from the old radio evangelistic programs and crusades of times past. Televangelism is one of the saddest things to happen to Christianity today as televangelists frequently concentrate on doctrines which are not part of the Bible. Televangelism also is one of the best things to happen as there are many very good God fearing televangelists who work hard to bring a solid program to listeners. Still, most televangelists can not discern between the Tribe of Judah and the House of Israel which are separate kingdoms on the earth at this time. To them, Judah is the whole house of Israel. This is not so. We must ask, do televangelists not know the difference between the House of Israel (known today as the Lost Tribes of Israel) and the tribe of Judah? It would seem so!

It appears as if the focus, for the most part, is more on making money and fame for the TV preacher than it is in presenting God's message to the world. It could be, and probably at one time was, instrumental in broadcasting the real Christian gospel truths to all of us while we could sit in the comfort of our own home. Now, some of it is more of an entertainment show laced with a little comedy. Some televangelism is still good, but lots of it is corrupt in that it teaches the subtly of Satan over Christianity under the guise if traditions. The number one goal in televangelism should be to convince you of the mission of God and that he has given us all the command to preach the gospel to all creatures.

Many televangelists carry the title of doctor which they think will cause you to revere them even more. And we would expect one with an advanced title to know more about the doctrines of Christianity than the average minister would know. However, this is not necessarily true as the college or seminary trained ministers concentrate on the beliefs of the school from which they graduate. One TV show about prophecy has nothing but doctors - the teacher on there is always using doctor this and doctor that and tries to prove his prophecies by such superiority minded tactics. Does he think we are awe struck by doctors? We are not! Remember this is the time when knowledge has been increased. We've been given the tools and intelligence to look through some false ideas which people are pushing in our way.

Some televangelists are shown in fancy settings with Hollywood props and wearing the very best in attire, including the ever present tailored thousand dollar suits, imported shoes, and their salon style hair done up in the latest fashion, etc. The focus is more on the televangelist than on the message he or she is attempting to teach.

Some televangelists use the timeworn scare tactics of doomsday messages to keep your attention rather than preaching the good news of God. They are constantly prophesying about things that are going to happen soon. It seldom ever happens and their message is altered or diverted into something new. No, it's not about the real hard truths of the Bible. They keep altering their themes. Some spend their entire career teaching the rapture theory which we have proven to be false. Some like to overpower your thinking with a constant ongoing staccato of scripture references with which one can hardly keep up to prove how knowledgeable they are. This is nothing but showmanship. We're talking about big name doctor preachers that feel like they know it all and expect you to feel the same. Most people in this day and age are not overwhelmed and awed by big names; as some of those with the heavy titles seem to know less about scripture than the everyday intelligent being.

One creation evangelist used to carry a plastic model of a dinosaur claiming Noah had dinosaurs on the ark! It's obvious a dinosaur could not fit on the ark! If you've ever been to a natural history museum and viewed the skeleton of a dinosaur, you would be shocked at the size of this pre-historic animal. One such museum in Denver displayed a dinosaur and it was very huge - taller and longer than a house. Noah was to take two of each species of animals on the ark. Considering the size of the ark with the size of the dinosaur, there would hardly be room for one baby dinosaur not to mention the amount of provender (food) that the dinosaur would need. Noah would have to have had three or four ark sized boats trailing behind with all the food a dinosaur would need for such a length of time as the flood - not to mention the large amounts of waste caused by the dinosaur. And don't dinosaurs have relatives who lived on earth in their time. Plainly, dinosaurs are animals from the first earth age.

Medical doctors like to get you into their office and amplify your deficiencies to scare you to death and load you down with pills.   Doesn't the TV preacher in lots of cases do the same.Think about this folks! You're frequently being taught a version of gospel principles or traditions which may or may not be Biblically based. The evangelist or cleric tries to makes you think you're going straight to hell if you disagree with his version of the Gospel; or for not sending money to support his ministry.

Then there's the doctor televangelist who thinks you are wor-shipping idols if you have a car in the garage, and a nice house and money in the bank. While we know of many people who own cars, have a nice house and money in the bank, we haven't seen any of them worshipping a car or their home. It is neces-sary in this day and age to own a car for transportation to and from your workplace. Also, a family must have a place to live as well as money in the bank to enable them to buy the necessi-ties of life. This does in no way constitute idol worship. These are things everybody needs. We must spend time keeping these necessary items in working order so they will last. Should you see a person shining a car or working in the rose garden and trimming around the house, this would in no way be idol worship. The true meaning of the gospel has been lost with such as this. The televangelist likely, after delivering the message, went to the parking lot and got into his BMW or Cadillac and drove to his high priced home.

He sells books and CDs on a timely basis and collects the inflated cost plus shipping and handling and you also send in your "love gift" which he has convinced you that you must do. Congratulations Slave! These same preachers flit around the country in their very own private jets planes, stay at the best hotels and eat the best gourmet foods available which people such as you have paid for! They brag about this! And you may be driving a beat up old Chevy or Ford. They like to be treated as royalty! Don't you think you've been had? Did Jesus teach this?

No, he taught exactly the opposite in Matthew 10:9-10:

"Provide neither gold, nor silver, nor brass in your purses,

"Nor scrip for your journey, neither two coats, neither shoes nor yet staves: for the workman is worthy of his meat"

We question the motive and honesty of some of our televangelists and wonder why they do what they do. They, and only they, can deal with this, but we must use our own God given knowledge and experience which in most instances would guide us to the right path and avoid costly mistakes. There are many good teachers of the Bible today and of course some of them are televangelists.

We have watched one televangelist who is very comical; and he relates his visit to heaven where he has seen God and Jesus and others who are abiding in heaven. He describes some people he has seen and talked to there including Daniel.

According to John 1:18: "No man has seen God at any time." How can one claim a visit to heaven with the apostle of Christ proclaiming the facts that no one has seen God at any time? As we have stated previously, the Gospel of Jesus Christ is not about escapades of man, nor about his possessions such as airplanes and his mansion on earth.

Conclusion

Although we have covered to some extent the doctrines and phenomenon of today's churches, the main focus of this writing is to call your attention to the latter day prophecies concerning the Tribes of Israel and your own heritage as a descendant of the modern day Israel.

Should you undertake a thorough study into the prophecies written in the Holy Bible concerning Israel, you must have a good understanding of where Israel is located today Prophets throughout the Bible have given descriptions of the future or latter day locations of Israel within the framework of specific prophecies.

Most prophets have placed Israel as a scattered people and located them in the Isles of Sea as well as their occupation in several nations of the world. Some of today's Bible teachers and clergy indicate Israel is no longer in existence or they are in today's tiny Israel in the Palestinian area. This premise is emphatically not true! We need only remember prophecies regarding the size of Israel - as massive as the sands of the sea! Rebekah, the wife of Isaac, was told in her patriarchal blessing that her descendents would be numbered in the thousands of millions! There are less than six million Jews living in the nation today known as Israel.

The Prophecies will locate Israel for you. We urge you to read Amos 9:9 and Ezekiel 37: 15-23. We have talked throughout this book about Israel being located in America, Great Britain, and most European nations. Israel is still divided into tribes and is still very much alive residing in all nations of the earth!

The full Twelve Tribes of Israel will be reunited in their former home in Palestine when God returns to set up his Kingdom on earth.

Printed in the United States
50920LVS00002B/271-306

9 781598 004151